ROME WORKS

*An Architect Explores the World's Most
Resilient City*

TOM RANKIN

Peruzzi Press

Published by: Peruzzi Press (www.peruzzipress.com)

Printed in the United States of America

First Printing, 2015

ISBN 978-0692559413

CONTENTS

PREFACE

This book is an account of over two decades of life in Rome, observing the city, learning about it everyday, and working humbly in hopes of making it an even better place. Some of the content will be familiar to readers of the *Still Sustainable City Blog,* but much is new and written from memory, which is known to play tricks. There are probably inaccuracies, which I am happy to fix in future editions, but I sincerely hope I haven't painted an erroneous picture of Rome — or of anyone of its players — in these pages. If so, please drop me a line at tom@romeworks.net and I will make amends.

-Tom Rankin

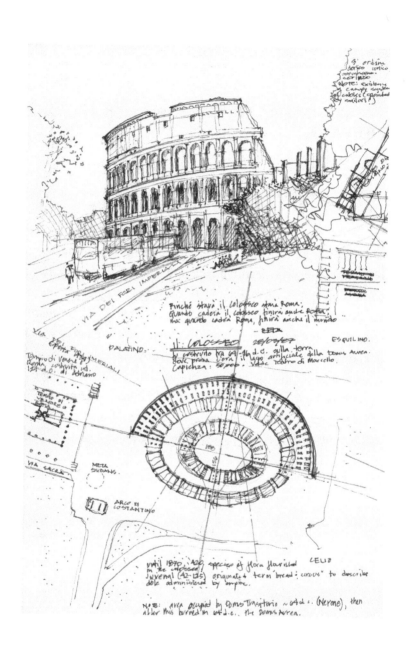

"The greatest function of the city is to encourage the greatest possible number of meetings, encounters, challenges, between varied persons and groups, providing... a stage upon which the drama of social life may be enacted."
-Lewis Mumford

INTRODUCTION: WHY ROME?

First Impressions

The train, as I recall, is on time. It pulls slowly into Termini Station, the screeching of brakes giving way to the echoing announcements of departures and delays. Passengers arriving from Tuscany, Lombardy or beyond begin to merge into the cosmopolitan chaos of Rome. I say goodbye to new acquaintances, a handful of backpackers like myself, a quiet Franciscan priest and a boisterous, bearded political science student who had been eager to share anti-American and anti-clerical sentiments but was frustrated by the language barrier.

From the train window I watched as green fields and rolling hills abruptly gave way to massive urban apartment blocks. Fleeting glimpses of private lives floated by. Balconies, dim interiors seen through open windows, bright sheets hung in the sun, a child on a balcony, an old man in a white undershirt smoking, an overgrown garden, a junkyard filled with wrecked cars, a Roman wall. Actually, it's *the* Roman wall, the Aurelian Wall, and one of its gates, the Porta Maggiore. Above I see the cross-sections of ancient aqueducts and peer in passing into concrete corridors which once carried Rome's water. Then, alongside another stretch of aqueducts I glimpse a broken octagonal dome and recognize the ruins of the ancient Temple of Minerva Medica. Before the train has begun braking, I am overwhelmed.

Now in the station, descending the narrow steps, a stench like old public restrooms rises from the litter-strewn tracks and blends with the smoke of freshly lit cigarettes. Why the sudden need to light up, I wonder; everyone had been smoking in the aisle of the train for the whole trip. (This was 1983, long before smoking bans reached Italy.)

I pause on the platform to let first impressions form. As the smoke clears I observe the crisp, repetitive lines of the station's mosaic-faced concrete canopies that frame the deep-blue October sky. The late afternoon sun is warm but I move several steps into the shade and feel its cooling effect. Then I hear the water. It bubbles continuously like a tiny mountain spring from a black basalt stone fountain, elegantly incorporated into the base of the dark stone piers. I stoop to drink and the water is cold and sweet.

Slow Architecture

I am an architect who feels little need to build. For every one thousand Italians there are approximately two architects, one every two square kilometers. Rome alone has 18,000 architects, a stable population, and a stock of buildings that has been growing, on and off, for millennia. The city which I have called home for two decades has many needs, but new architecture is not foremost among them.

The challenge today is not growth but restraint, not building more but using better that which we have, not reinventing the city but rethinking how we *live* the city[1].

Cities use about 75 percent of the earth's resources and produce the same percentage of greenhouse emissions. But this doesn't mean, as previous generations suggested, that the solution to our global crisis is to abandon the city. If, as some environmentalists once suggested, we commune with nature, we risk destroying the very wilderness that we claim to cherish. No, we are urban animals and the city is our nature. From environmentalists to urbanists to administrators, people are finally waking up to the realization that, if we can fix our cities, we stand at least a chance of fixing our planet.

At the start of the modern era cities were, often rightly, depicted as concentrations of pollution, injustice and waste, but this is no longer true. As our industries have gone from grey to green (or moved to distant shores, which is another story) most of the negative consequences of urbanism have vaporized. Instead cities offer the best–perhaps the only–venue in which to build a new economy that, in Lester Brown's words, is powered largely by renewable sources of energy, boasts a much more diversified transport system, and that reuses and recycles everything.

So if "cities aren't the problem, they are the solution," as Jamie Lerner, the former mayor of Curitiba, Brazil, has succinctly put it, we should look carefully at Rome, the quintessential city. It may no longer be Caput Mundi, as the Romans saw it, but there is perhaps no more archetypal city in the world, making it an important laboratory for the inevitable transition which world cities will undergo if they are to survive.

Rome's Termini Station during Critical Mass bike ride

Cities not Built from Scratch

With a nearly three-thousand year head-start on the "cities from scratch" materializing on the screens of visionary architects like Norman Foster, Rome contains an urban complexity which cannot be cultivated quickly. The very persistence of Rome's physical structure over time, transformed, renewed, enlarged and sometimes downsized, has allowed Rome to achieve cultural prosperity while minimizing material and energy expenditures. When we get beyond the green rhetoric of the newest technological solutions in solar collectors and UV glass, the greenest building is usually one which has already been built, thus eliminating the environmental costs of its demolition and reconstruction.

We tend to think of Rome as a city that fell, that ended, that had its day, like an old refrigerator that we send to the landfill, but contemporary Rome refutes this. In Rome we are reminded that cities are not like old cars that fulfill their increasingly short useful lives and are then discarded and replaced. They persist, transformed, as needs, limitations, technologies and users change. Cultural production, like biodiversity, unless interfered with has a tendency to get more sophisticated over time and in Rome this has been going on with peaks and valleys for millennia. In Rome we see that cities, like nature, are more resilient than anyone thought possible.

An Olivetti and Lots of Fiats

Since the end of the Second World War Italy had been focused on reconstruction and on finding its place on the international stage. In doing so, two contrasting traditions were at work. On the one hand there was a sense of public service, of joining forces to rebuild a war-damaged country. Master plans for new towns sprouted from the drawing boards of planning commissions. Gone now was the monumentality of the Fascist new towns. The postwar urban designers sought to achieve a collective sense through pseudo-vernacular language (peaked roofs, iron railings, etc.) and informal, shared public spaces. Many of these new towns and new urban neighborhoods were financed under the INA-Casa project, a national insurance company with the capital needed to jump start growth. The U.S. government also provided support, both financial and advisory, especially through the United States Information Service which helped produced the *Manuale del Architetto*. This veritable building manual, still on the bookshelves of most Italian architects over forty, provided instructions and templates for traditional and modern construction. The construction industry boomed in mid-century Italy and by the 1970's MIT social scientist Charles F. Sabel would find a "radically new way of organizing industrial society" in Italy's networks of small, innovative productive firms.

Meanwhile, Adriano Olivetti was making strides anticipating personal computing through cutting-edge business machines but also rethinking the workplace model by providing innovative campus-like facilities in the corporate headquarters in Ivrea, where employees would be encouraged to think creatively.

It was a time of frugality, by necessity. G. E. Kidder-Smith describes Italy's scarcity of resources: "almost no coal for heat, almost no iron for steel, no petroleum for movement, not enough forest products for paper and construction, not enough agricultural products for 47,000,000 mouths....rarely has so much genius flowered on such inhospitable ground.[2]"

This frugality was celebrated in film and literature, and to a degree in architecture, under the banner of neorealism. A decade later poet and film-maker Pier Paolo Pasolini would find in Rome's marginalized urban underclass inspiration for books such as *Ragazzi di Vita* and films like *Mamma Roma* and *Accatone*.

Rome's Aqueduct Park with INA-Casa housing where parts of Pasolini's Mamma Roma were filmed

But another Italy also thrived in the climate of uncertainty of the post-war years, an Italy of special interests, in which it was every man for himself and his family. In contrast to what Sabel saw, a much bleaker picture is painted by Ed Banfield in *The Moral Basis of a Backward Society*, one of "the inability of villagers to act together for the common good[3].

All the status symbols for this other Italy seem to emanate directly from America: the automobile, the color TV, the shopping mall, and the single-family home.

Over the last thirty years in Italy I have witnessed the struggle for Italy's civic heritage to hold its own against the onslaught of private interests. Another way to view this struggle is between planning and regulation, on the one hand, and unregulated, often illegal, action, a struggle which has taken its toll on the global economy and the natural environment alike in recent decades. As an American in Rome I feel some responsibility for exposing the devastation that is being wrought on the eternal city in the name of neo-liberal progress. I've seen where it leads, and it isn't pretty.

Pastels and Solar Panels

My first trip to Rome coincided with the tail end of the *anni di piombo*, the "years of lead" named for the frequent shootings and violent unrest which left its mark on the streets of many Italian cities. As violence raged on the streets of Rome in the late seventies I was just starting to study the great works of Western culture. For four years in the manicured grounds of Princeton University I learned to draw buildings and follow the timeless compositional rules of classicism. I also learned a great deal about the masterpieces of architectural history, a large number of which seemed to be in Italy. Architecture schools in the early eighties, in particular Princeton under the reign of Michael Graves, were preaching a return to history, especially the 19th century neoclassical Beaux-Arts style, known by the moniker "post-modernism". It was refreshing after decades of dry and pedantic modernist excess to see a human touch in buildings. History was again okay, as was a bit of ornament if the budget allowed. It was fun to make buildings with facades that attracted — rather than offended— the masses and with plans that followed straightforward rules of connectivity. The rules of the game and its playing pieces were easy to pick up and I turned out to be a pretty good player. Axes, symmetry, hierarchy, an insider's game built around buzzwords like parti' and *poché* produced surprisingly believable results on paper. Rendered in pastel *prismacolor* pencils, the effect was mesmerizing.

And yet this game felt wrong.

Outside of the design studio, I was active in the nascent environmental movement, participating in committees to fight nuclear proliferation, pollution and the military-industrial complex. With my small group of friends at Princeton I would read E.F. Schumacher's *Small is Beautiful* and Leo Marx's *The Machine in the Garden*. I became a vegetarian, cooking big pots of rice and veggies with stoned intellectuals while rocking out to Patti Smith or Funkadelic. My desk was covered with clippings about alternative energy technologies, usually awkward-looking contraptions jerry-rigged from solar panels, inverters and arrays of batteries assembled, it would seem, by hippies in Vermont or Germany and sold through mail order companies advertised in the back of Rodale magazine or the Whole Earth Catalogue. While I found the new-age self-righteousness hard to stomach, I was convinced that architecture could provide an alternative to our high-impact, consumptive lifestyle.

In the architecture schools of the 1980s however, with the possible exception of Berkeley or MIT, voicing a concern for sustainability was met with eye-rolling normally reserved for bell-bottoms or tie-died t-shirts. Here we were reading Michel Foucault and Aldo Rossi, looking to the city and its architecture to provide systems of signs, structures and stories. Architecture was language and form. I might prefer the creative atmosphere of the design school, and the Talking Heads and Tom-Tom-Club were certainly more danceable than the folk-rock of the whole earth crowd, but it was clear that I was not going to even utter the word "sustainability" without disparagement.

I was fortunate to find the sympathetic ear and inspiring advice of a professor in the engineering school (where being cool was not even an option) to advise me. With Professor Steve Slaby, and Architecture Dean Robert Maxwell who bravely stepped up to the plate as second reader, I wrote my thesis on "ecological urbanism" in the native pueblo villages of the American Southwest. Environmentalism and archaeology, a less fashionable option could not have been conceived.

Years later the pendulum has swung; history is now out of fashion and sustainability is the buzz word even in schools that shunned it decades ago. Green is the new black.

Rome Revisited

Not quite two years after Princeton, having earned a bit of money and some practical experience lending my post-modern design skills and European precedents to speculative real-estate developers at architectural firms in Boston, I am back in Italy. This time I have budgeted a full two weeks for Rome and its environs. In hindsight, far from satisfying my desire to "do" Rome this must have been the fatal decision that would hook me permanently. I found a city of clunky Fiats and Alfas and lots of two-stroke Piaggio motor scooters spewing black smoke on streets crowded with craftspeople, shopkeepers, bureaucrats, students, clergy, a few tourists and even fewer immigrants. Except for the favorable exchange rate, Rome was not an easy place for the traveler, nor a particularly pleasant one. But for a penniless architecture student with a sketchbook, it was perfect. Great palaces I recognized from slide lectures were covered in grime and graffiti and, if not semi-abandoned, usually filled with dusty smoke-filled offices of obscure government departments.

Each evening I would plan the following day's exploration, often with an Irish architecture student named Gavin I had met in my *pensione* near the train station. He had Bannister Fletcher, I had the Atlas of European Architecture, a book that I still use for its minimalist logic in combining a chronological list of buildings with nothing but the essential information with gray scale label-less maps overlaid with tiny numbers. Every day I would systematically observe, photograph and sketch Rome's built heritage.

Two weeks flew by and I was off to Germany (or was it Spain?) but I would never rid myself of the passion for Rome I developed in those two short weeks. Every other city would be lacking. Not enough contrast, too flat, too self-consciously efficient, too contained or too sprawling. Back in Boston after four months exploring the old continent, from London to Jerusalem, it was Rome that most often filled my daydreams.

As an architectural designer beginning to work in architectural firms in my home city of Boston, fresh out of college, I had found myself involved in projects of various scales where the basic structures and systems had already been dictated by economic and policy factors. I was usually tasked only with the application of aesthetic expression, the icing on the cake. I was more interested then, as I am today, in design as a means to achieve synergies and efficiencies, to create flexible frameworks for a wide range of potential future scenarios, and the challenges facing Rome involve just that.

And it was to Rome that I would return again and again until one day, practically without realizing it, I found I had become an expat. I continued to travel between the US and Italy, but now it was to return home to America to visit my aging parents, to renew my own children's sense of their American heritage, and to shop for books, electronics and cheap clothing which were still rare in Italy.

Welcome to the Real World

From my expat vantage point, I was no longer able to believe some impossible *bella vita* under the Roman sun now that I was dealing with it on a daily basis, nor would I let stand the stereotypes many Italians harbored about America, either to idealize or to vilify it. All that was left was to share my unique perspective in hopes that I could lend insight to Romans and outsiders alike. I had one foot in the architectural milieu, mired in its dense history and muddy theorizing, rich and seductive but with surprisingly little relevance, especially since I was in no position to win international competitions which might, by some remote turn of events, have spelled success for me (as opposed to Rome's other 18,000 architects or, for that matter, any of the world's millions of architects who would give their right arm to build in Rome). If I had one foot in architecture, my other foot was in the real world. And this world, one of emerging global opportunities, fueled by digital media and communications, seemed inextricably linked to a cycle of production and consumption that led straight to planetary catastrophe.

Or did it? Kenneth Frampton argues convincingly for a critical regionalism, for architecture as a force of resistance against what he calls universal civilization. Places, grounded in history, topography, hydrology, places like Rome, might act as anti-entropic forces against the momentum of dumbed down globalization.

In Rome I found these two worlds, that of culture and history on the one hand and that of urban ecology on the other, able to coexist. Over time (lots of it!) the city gradually emerged reinforced by feedback loops, positive and negative both. Pushing outwards, driven by internal forces usually wielded by an economic elite though on occasion, such as the revolt of the Plebes in the 2nd century BCE, with grassroots instigation. But also limited by external constraints: the Tiber river, the seven hills, the Apennine Mountains, the Mediterranean Sea, availability of food, land and building materials.

Lewis Mumford, in his seminal work *The City in History*, writes that our first task in our attempt to achieve a better insight into the present state of the city, is to "peer over the edge of the historic horizon, to detect the dim traces of still earlier structures and more primitive functions." Certainly he had Rome in mind. Rome, more than most other cities, has seen a persistent and continuous process of expansion and retraction. Never completed, it is, like "modernism," an unfinished project. Yet, unlike instrumental functionalism striving toward some ideal "complete" state, Rome has accepted its flux as the condition of urbanism.

Rome as a Laboratory for Environmental Sustainability

To speak of environmental sustainability and Rome in the same sentence, or even the same book, may seem surprising. By various standards, Rome is dragging its feet in meeting goals such as reducing its dependence on fossil fuels, eliminating waste of water and other materials, and improving air quality by cutting emissions. In recent years Legambiente's *Ecosistemma Italia* report ranked Rome 75th out of 103 Italian cities it rated for sustainable practices, down from 62nd place in previous years.

At a time when many nations, as they pursue their increasing commitment to sustainable city building, are looking for lessons from the past in the traditional urbanism to Rome and other Italian cities, contemporary Rome itself has drifted in the other direction: toward forms urbanization that have been shown elsewhere to be unsustainable in other cultures, especially the US.

In place of the tradition of dense pedestrian and transit-oriented neighborhoods Rome has promoted peripheral dormitory and shopping developments, still only tenuously connected to the city except by private automobile.

The 2003 master plan for Rome, in an expressed effort to jump-start the polycentric organization of the city, called for 18 *centralità urbane e metropolitane*, mono-functional developments with commercial, educational or cultural programs. It is up to the next generation of designers, entrepreneurs, policymakers and citizens to see that these evolve into pieces of city and not just urbanized areas, a distinction that is fundamental. At a time when the planet is increasingly urban the qualities of cities are changing. As urban population has boomed, the average density of cities has decreased. Are we really becoming more urban?

In Rome, the current trends call into question the city's much flaunted resilience. In a city built upon centuries of adaptive reuse of both buildings and materials, there is serious discussion of demolition of massive structures such as Corviale, the infamous kilometer-long public housing project, and Tor Bella Monica. Reusable *sanpietrini* cobblestones are being replaced with throwaway asphalt. In a city which in antiquity demonstrated a clear understanding of passive solar heating and natural ventilation, few buildings of the past two decades can be said to have been designed on principals of solar thermal heating or cooling. In a city which can still boast one of the largest percentages of agricultural land within its boundaries, each year thousands of acres of fertile soil are being given over to urbanization. A city which in the post-war years developed not just a network but a culture of buses and trams now has the highest per capita private automobile usage in Europe. And, last but not least, a capital whose rise to power was thanks in great part to an abundant and equitably distributed water supply is now moving towards the privatization of that water. It is enough to look around Rome (or read numerous Rome-based public advocacy blogs) to dismiss any notion that the eternal city today is a model of ecological urbanism. That title might go to Vancouver or Copenhagen, to Curitiba, even London or here in Italy to Siena (n. 6 on Legambiente list), but not to Rome.

But I am suggesting Rome not as a model but as a laboratory, that is a venue in which to carry out research, to "work on problems" as the etymology of the word reminds us. A laboratory is a place where scientific work gets done. In her last book, *Dark Age Ahead*, one of the world's great urban thinkers, Jane Jacobs, praises (or eulogizes?) the scientific method through which a fruitful question is posed, a hypothetical answer proposed, then tested, leading to the next fruitful question. It is through such rigorous work, not through heroic gestures, that the hard problems are solved and the species evolves.

Science and design are often seen as opposites, the former wide open to all knowledge while the latter invariably narrows down the choices to one out of infinite possibilities, one color, one choice But when it comes to the study of the city, science and culture comprise a unified field of inquiry.

The late Italian architect Aldo Rossi, author of one of the landmark architectural texts of the last century, *The Architecture of the City*, often slipped the term "scientific" into his discourse: the scientific autobiography, the little scientific theatre, etc. Italian examples of science and culture finding common ground or at least promiscuity abound: Vitruvius, Hadrian, the Arcadian movement, the Academy of the Lincei, Giordano Bruno, Enrico Fermi, Renzo Piano, and the list could go on. Even the presence in Rome of NGOs such as the Food and Agricultural Organization (FAO) and the World Food Program point to the city's ambiguous position between science and public policy, between the global north and south. Sadly we are in a period in which both culture and scientific research are under attack, their funding being cut, undermining seriously the sustainable future of Italian society. Jane Jacobs' discussion of the scientific method, in fact, pointed to cases in which it is being abandoned by the very people, such as "traffic engineers," who purport to carry its torch.

Seven Themes

This book is structured around seven themes, like the seven early kings of Rome or the seven hills on which they founded the city. Like Rome itself, these themes overlap and sometimes contradict one another (is the Pantheon a classical temple or an early Christian church, a feat of engineering or a humanist hangout?). Nevertheless they will serve as useful organizational devices to reign in the complex history of a complex city.

Rome at the start of the 21st century is at a tipping point, on the verge of falling again by abandoning a long, rich and deeply established tradition and instead adopting some of the worst aspects of American culture. And if it falls this time, it may not get back up. What's worse is that if Rome can't resist these superficial temptations, how can we expect China to? However, in each of the seven sustainability themes presented here Rome could just as easily turn its efforts toward sustainable urban design and become not just a laboratory but a world model for urban sustainability.

Notes

1. I am paraphrasing here the teachings of Professor Francesco Scoppola.

2. G.E.Kidder-Smith, Italy Builds (New York: Reinhold Publishing Co.; 2nd Printing 1957) 16.

3. Ed Banfield, The Moral Basis of a Backward Society (Free Press, 1967) 55.

CHAPTER 1.

WATER: ACQUA BENE PUBBLICO

Walking through the caked mud, weeds and scattered refuse which litters the Tiber River's left bank, you encounter few tourists, even here, just downstream from the Tiber Island, in the heart of Rome. High above you flows a river of cars, trucks, buses and scooters, one of central Rome's only continuous traffic arteries, but the noise of traffic stays up there, kept at bay by the massive travertine embankment wall as high as a four-story building. Just above you, tourists view the circular Temple of Hercules Victor, the first Roman temple to be made of Greek marble, or the slightly earlier temple to Portunus, the Roman god of keys, gates, and, later, ports. Or perhaps they head to the

8th-century Basilica of Santa Maria in Cosmedin, also nearby, drawn to the *Bocca della Verità* in its portico. Once a drain plate in the form of a face mask, this stone disk now serves as a famously kitsch backdrop for a selfie. But a few intrepid travelers dare to dart through the speeding traffic and gaze down over the thick stone parapet into the slow-flowing, muddy river.

Where they are standing once stood the sloping riparian banks and later, during the early Republic, bustling port facilities replete with docks, warehouses, and a multitude of temples. The last remnants of these vanished in the late 19th century, when the nascent Italian capital, tired of frequent flooding, undertook the massive public works project that would end the flooding forever. At least that was the idea.

Apart from the occasional jogger or fisherman (fishing for what in this dirty water you ask yourself?) you are alone down here at the river's edge. Ducks and cormorants slip through the river grasses; Saxifraga and the occasional elm tree grow out of the rocky banks. You may see a nutria, looking something like a large rat or small beaver, a species imported in the 1950s from South America—their meat was thought to be a delicacy, and their fur was used in clothing—then released into the wild when the farms that bred them failed.

The air is humid. As the river rushes around the Tiber Island, a mist often arises from the rapids and small waterfalls on either side. You continue downstream past the remains of the *Pons Aemilius* (later called, for obvious reasons, *Ponte Rotto*, or broken bridge), and then under the high iron trusses of the *Ponte Palatino*, and before long a section of the path you are on *itself* becomes a bridge. Below you, through a gap in the luxuriant vegetation in the embankment wall, you spy a heavy yellowish-grey stone arch. You have stumbled upon the outlet of ancient

Rome's first permanent engineered structure, the sewer main known to us as the *Cloaca Maximus.*

If it has rained recently you will see water gushing from the stone arch into the river. In the dry summer months, when this is reduced to a trickle, the cavernous opening in the embankment wall becomes an impromptu homeless shelter. It is common to see laundry drying on the fence protecting the drain, or t-shirts and tattered sleeping bags draped along this monument to Roman engineering.

Most people expect the first monument of Rome to have been a temple or a palace or perhaps a defensive wall, but the *Cloaca Maximus* is little more than a mundane sewer pipe. Since its inauguration in the 6th century BCE it has been channeling storm water and runoff from the low-lying wetlands into the Tiber River. The original cutting for the Cloaca in the 6th century BCE, John Hopkins writes, was part of a larger landfill project "intended to change Rome's urban space in a monumental fashion.[1]" The open drainage channel was covered in the 2nd century BCE by massive arches of local tuff stone, nearly 5 meters in diameter.

Lewis Mumford has calculated that, were the initial cost of the Cloaca to be amortized over its 2,000 year (and counting) useful life, it would prove one of the world's most cost-effective public works projects.[2]

Going Underground

Unlike some enterprising, fortunate or foolhardy friends of mine, I have never put on scuba equipment to explore the ancient tunnels of the Cloaca Maximus. My friend Paul Bennett, who investigated the great drain for an article published in *National*

Geographic, describes the odor as..."a mélange of urine, diesel, mud, and rotting rat carcasses.[3]" I don't regret sitting out that adventure.

I have, however, crawled through the much smaller drainage channels hidden below the Roman Forum in the area of the Temple of Castor and Pollux. As the primary architect for the *Post Aedem Castoris* project in 2004, I was quick to volunteer to explore them. The project was jointly conducted by a team of archaeologists from Stanford and Oxford universities, and a non-profit organization I had cofounded.

Our purpose then was to explore theories about the location of the Temple of Augustus, which touched in turn upon a larger question about Caligula's palace. Students of Roman history have long questioned whether the historian Seutonius was serious when he wrote that Caligula had "built out a part of the Palace as far as the Forum ...making the temple of Castor and Pollux its vestibule." Given they were not the most modest rulers, but what emperor would go so far as to requisition one of Rome's most venerated sites for his front door? And what of the paved street that sources describe as separating the temple from the hill before Caligula's reign (37-41 AD), part of which Giacomo Boni unearthed in hasty excavations a century ago?

The absence of any visible remains of Caligula's palace—if indeed such a structure existed—is hardly surprising, however. No emperor, it is commonly acknowledged, deserved less to be remembered than the one whose depravities, Seutonius wrote, included fratricide, incest, and ruthless killing of anyone who piqued his wrath. The list Seutonius made of instances of Caligula's "innate brutality" is long, but one stands out: "He had the manager of his gladiatorial shows and beast baitings beaten with chains in his presence for several successive days, and would not kill him until he was disgusted at the stench of his putrefied brain." Nice guy, this Caligula, and not surprising that his successors recalled his reign with less than a warm heart. The Roman Senate instead passed a *Damnatio Memoriae*—an official condemnation and erasure of his name from history.

But erasing all visible traces of Caligula's hated palace didn't include the invisible: buried below the surface, the perimeter drains remained and are now clues as to what may have been above.

As I crawl on all fours through them, the narrow, labyrinthine tunnels are just wide enough for my shoulders. And so low that I keep banging my hard-hat on the *bipedales*, the over-sized bricks set in pairs to form a simple but functional, peaked ceiling. After thousands of years I expected the system to be filled with rubble and vegetation, but I found only small animal and bird bones crunching under my hands and knees. During the rainy season, the very flow of water keeps this system clean, pushing the city's detritus out to the Tiber and from there on to the sea. Another instance of Roman pragmatism I must pause to salute, and I have encountered many in my years in Rome. The channel is built to last, slightly oversized to anticipate future expansion and weather extremes but with the assumption that future generations would build with comparable common sense. If water is to be mastered we must respect it and, with a proper understanding of its properties and limitations, channel it in the direction it wants to go. From the earliest archaeological evidence we have, the primitive cabanas on the Palatine hill, the so-called hut of Romulus, perimeter drains are in evidence. And it was not much later that they began to channel rain water into cisterns for civic use. Even long after the buildings above ceased to function, water continues to flow through these drains (except, thankfully, in the dry summer months when our investigation took place.)

I continued my sewer crawl, trying to construct a rough map in my head as the channel twisted and turned a few times and the sounds of the Roman Forum became ever more distant. My hopes of finding a space wide enough to turn around dimmed and the anticipation of backing all the way out — not to mention irrational fears of flash floods or earthquakes — began loom over me. I soon stopped, took a deep breath, and reversed my direction. With perseverance and proper equipment — and more courage than I could muster — I might have followed a course through the gradually widening channels until emerging into the sunlight at the Tiber's edge, where our story began.

Biking along the Tiber riverfront

Off-site, Out of Mind

Italy is filled with such conduits, though none are so historically loaded. In Tuscany, under the Etruscan town of Chiusi, there is an extensive network of tunnels, called the Labyrinth of Porsenna, which you enter through a garden along the medieval town walls. You eventually find yourself in a tall Roman cistern, from which you ascend by means of a seemingly endless spiral stairway until you emerge, breathless, onto the vertiginous bell-tower of the town's cathedral. The cavernous tunnels are a bit like Rome's Christian catacombs, but made to hold water, not the remains of martyrs.

They made me think of William Mitchell's description, in his book *Me++*, of the tangled mess of metal and plastic that snakes beneath the contemporary metropolis. "Water supply and sewer networks," he writes, "have become geographic extensions of my alimentary canal, my respiratory system, and associated organic plumbing.[4]" The labyrinth below Chiusi can induce a similar hallucination: you begin to wonder if you've shrunk to Lilliputian size and are somehow wandering around inside Gulliver's biological plumbing. You snap to, however, as you realize that our cities have indeed long since developed plumbing systems not unlike those of living organisms, though probably less resilient.

The perimeter drains I explored in 2004, and the ones under Chiusi, were originally covered. They had gratings through which water could pass and entrances for maintenance workers. But the Cloaca Maxima was as open-air canal whose primary aim was to create firm ground out of former wetlands by separating wet from dry.

Today we hide our infrastructure, letting it do its work silently in the background as we slip into ignorance of the resources on which we depend. Our waste quickly disappears out of sight at the push of a button, only returning to plague us when the technology breaks down. Normally, the contaminated byproducts of our consumptive lifestyles are shipped away to distant destinations, out of sight, out of mind. Where does your water come from? Where does your waste end up when you flush, and where is this place called "away"? In ancient Rome, and in many other early cultures, people knew, and their answers were often quite specific. Indeed these essential solutions were celebrated—not hidden. When early Rome's dirty waste water passed in full view (and in a fully odiferous state) through the city, the ecological impact of its inhabitants was much harder to ignore. As William Mitchell reminds us, central plumbing, for good or ill, is invisible plumbing. The well and the outhouse, once outside our homes, are now replaced with sleek plumbing that is largely indistinguishable from the rest of our homes. "The large scale construction of these intestinal extranets," he writes, "and the integration of their interfaces into architecture were among the most heroic projects of early modernism."[5] Awareness of the importance of making the structural innards visible, even to the point of making it a fetish, informed projects like the Pompidou Center in central Paris. Designed in 1977 by the then-young architects Renzo Piano and Richard Rogers, the expressive high-tech building boasts exposed and colorfully highlighted ductwork. Yet the real revolution in our technology will be in its miniaturization and dematerialization. Despite noble (or at least theatrical) efforts to make visible the obscure systems which drive our cities, our infrastructure has again gone underground.

Navigating the Tiber and its Bureaucracy

In central Rome's vast waste removal system, the Cloaca Maxima is but one segment of its quintessential drain—the Tiber itself. Especially since the creation of its tall embankment walls at the end of the 19th century, Rome's river has been treated like one large sewer and its outlet, at the port of Ostia, has been increasingly polluted in recent years. The effects of Rome's river and others on the Mediterranean in turn threatens the aquatic ecosystem and Italy's fishing economy.

The Tiber River barely exists in the minds of most Romans, and yet it is *the* historic river of Europe, and where the city of Rome began. Specifically, it was at on its then-natural banks where the river winds past the base of the Palatine Hill, that the infant twins, Romulus and Remus were said to have washed ashore in a basket and been adopted by the legendary she-wolf. The city's official — though of course mythical — foundation by the now adult Romulus came in 753 BCE (April 21 to be precise) and since that day the history of Rome has been inextricably tied to the Tiber. The river served as a boundary, separating the north-western Etruscan tribes from the Latins in the southeast. Across the Tiber Island the first bridges were once built, first in wood and later in stone; one of them, the first century BCE Ponte Fabricio, still survives today. The river provides a connection to the sea, close enough for shipping but far enough upstream to prevent hostile incursions.

Watching the Tiber River as it snakes slowly through central Rome on its way to the Mediterranean, it is hard to conceive of the fuzzy web of interests and regulatory bodies at play. Shared amongst multiple authorities— a minimum of 16 administrative offices have a say in the river — the responsibilities often seem so contradictory and overlapping as to make any proposal for the river a daunting enterprise.

The *Regione Lazio*, one of the twenty regions of Italy, extending southwards half-way to Naples and towards Florence in the north, is responsible for the river and its banks, specifically under the management of ARDIS, *l'Agenzia Regionale per la Difesa del Suolo* (a regional agency for land management). But the Tiber doesn't stop at the city's edges, nor at those of the Lazio region. The river begins as a natural spring, bubbling out of the ground at Fiumarolo, in the Emilia Romagna region and gathering force as it winds through Umbria and Tuscany before entering Lazio, and each region along the way has a voice in its management.

The greatest overall responsibility for drafting and implementing an overall environmental plan (*Piano Paesistico*) for the entire river ecosystem is borne by the *Autorità di Bacino del Fiume Tevere*. Based near Rome's Termini Station, in a drab building the Castro Pretorio neighborhood , this authority drafted the current in 2003 plan and is currently overseeing its implementation. Any projects with potential impact on the Tiber River ecosystem must pass through these offices and receive, literally, a stamp of approval.

In case of hydrological emergencies still other authorities are called into play, coordinated by the national civil protection agency, *Protezione Civile*. La Polizia Fluviale, based strategically on the Tiber Island, sends two small boats up and downstream to check water levels and the condition of the embankments. The Capitaneria del Porto also plays an important role, especially at Fiumicino and Ostia, where the river enters the sea. Finally, because any interventions along the river may be architectural, environmental, cultural, recreational, or even social in nature, multiple commissioners are called upon to express their opinions.

One cultural and social engagement project, launched in the

early 2000s by the nonprofit organization Tevereterno Onlus, is aimed at revitalizing the urban riverfront by creating a public space dedicated to site-specific contemporary art. Supported by various international constituencies, from the art world to designers to environmentalists, this catalyst project has nevertheless struggled to gain recognition by administrative authorities. The river, instead, continues to lie forgotten beneath its tall stone walls, nearly abandoned but overflowing with potential as a public place.

High Water

Ever more frequently, the Tiber reaches upwards as heavy and continuous rainfall fills its delta, causing bridge closings and warnings by the city's mayor to stay home and providing gripping video clips for climate-change activists. On a recent day the water rose 5 meters in 2 days to surpass the springing points and start to fill the arches of ancient bridges such as Ponte Milvio and Ponte Fabricius. Boats moored near St. Peter's came loose and were washed into Ponte Sant'Angelo where they piled up and further obstructed the flow, threatening a structure that dates its founding to the time of Hadrian.

The Tiber has always flooded and it would be simplistic to point to this flood in particular as evidence of the worsening effects of global warning or even excessive urbanization of the river basin. Deforestation and subsequent erosion and flooding are as old as the Colosseum and plans for artificial diversion and channeling of the river go back to the time of Caesar.

Caesar's scheme would have involved cutting a canal from a point upstream and bypassing Rome to the east and south until emptying into the sea at Ostia. This project was again proposed in the 19th century, this time advocated by none other than the general and war hero, Giuseppe Garibaldi. A contemporary American newspaper article noted: "The project is practicable, and would be of great utility if carried out. But there is no capital to be found here for its execution.[6]" The hope of attaining foreign investors to fund the canal was never realized.

Instead, a Roman engineer named Raffaele Canevari proposed the embankment or *muraglioni*, a costly public works project which would result in the expropriation and demolition of many buildings and public spaces and the redesign of the entire urban waterfront along the Tiber banks. Dismantled and buried in the process were the *Porta di Ripetta*, Rome's most elegant river port (designed by Baroque architect Alessandro Specchi in the 18th century), the vibrant Porta di Ripa Grande in Trastevere and the entire former Jewish "Ghetto." Historic bridges such as Ponte Fabricio, Ponte Sisto and Ponte Sant'Angelo were trimmed to fit the narrower course of the Tiber. The solution worked, and has kept the river within its walls, but typical of the heavy-handed approach of the 19th century, it had a negative impact, separating the city from its river.

Today the problem of flooding derives less from the river and more from the impermeable surfaces which can translate heavy rains into flash flooding. There is no linear causality but rather a web of connectivity, but if we incorporated green space into our city-building, rains like this would be absorbed and enrich the aquifers, rather than overflowing into rivers. Likewise, our dependence on automobiles traps us in rising floodwaters, blocking emergency vehicles and public transit, effectively shutting down the city in situations where were we on foot, living close enough to our daily needs to walk, we might get wet but still function. During a recent summer storm, for example, I biked to work as usual (actually better than usual because the clogged

traffic meant that for once I wasn't a target of homicidal drivers).
I simply brought dry clothes and changed when I got to work.

Ponte Rotto and the Tiber island during the 2012 floods

When the floodwaters of the Tiber subside after the rainy season, plastic bags, bottles, shredded packaging materials, and other detritus draped from trees remind Romans and visitors of the forces of nature but also of our throw-away culture. Some might see in this display a valuable message. Non-biodegradable trash that is usually hidden from view in landfills to secretly intoxicate our land here hangs visible to all in all its ugliness, a glaring reminder of our wasteful society. Flushing the city's waste away is today a greater challenge than it was in antiquity, and this could provide a needed wake-up call.

Bringing in the Water

Centuries after resolving the problem of the elimination of unwanted groundwater with the Cloaca Maxima, Roman engineers applied the same logic, and the same laws of gravity and fluid dynamics, to the procurement of fresh water. Like the Cloaca, the majority of the aqueducts' extent is underground, only partially explored and excavated. The first aqueduct in Rome was the Acqua Appia, built in 312 BCE by the same Appius Claudius we will encounter later as the engineer of the first Roman highway. By the year 95, Sextus Julius Frontinus describes "nine aqueducts from which water converges into Rome," and by the time two others are added there would be a total of 470 kilometers of aqueducts, all but 70 km of it underground, carrying almost a billion liters of water into the capital each day. The increase in potable water was paralleled by an increase in population.[7] As Rome grew from a small city to a metropolis of over a million residents by the 3rd century, its water consumption reached an estimated 12,000 liters/second, a record not surpassed until the late 20th century, by which time its population had doubled. Of course, in between the fall of Rome and our own times 10 of the 11 aqueducts ceased to function and the population plummeted. The wellbeing of the city's residents was clearly tied to the supply of clean water.

Frontinus' text, *De Aquaeductu Urbis Romae* is the most authoritative voice regarding aqueducts to have survived and, together with extant structures, it is not hard to understand the functioning of ancient Rome's plumbing. For example, each aqueduct terminated in a Castellum, a sort of distribution tank from which smaller channels would continue to feed public fountains, public baths, and private homes or baths (in that order, so in the event of water shortage, the private users would be the first to suffer).

Frontinus makes it clear that water was used for more than just drinking and bathing. Vitruvius, writing almost a century earlier his own treatise about architecture in general, stated "without water, neither the body of an animal, nor even food itself can be raised, preserved, nor provided." As Vitruvius observed, "water is of infinite utility to us, not only as affording drink, but for a great number of purposes in life; and it is furnished to us gratuitously." Water irrigates our plants, and Rome then and now was a heavily agricultural society with an intimate awareness of the importance of water supplies on crop cycles. Water cleanses us, and flushes our cities of their waste, carrying dangerous toxins out to sea. The movement of water provides power for work such as the grinding of grain and, later, the production of electricity. Water also generates microclimatic conditions that benefit human inhabitation: the Mediterranean climate exists thanks to the thermal mass of the nearby sea, which reduces temperature extremes. At a localized level, water can serve for evaporative cooling or for heating. And, of course, water is a beautiful, sensual presence in our lives. It is no surprise that Frontinus said "springs are revered for their sanctity, and their water is thought to bring health to sick bodies." Today, in a world devastated by environmental injustice, the abundance of free, clean public water is one of Rome's most striking assets.

Nympheum

Romans nearly worship their water, as I learn on a hot summer day sometime in the early 1990s, when I first seriously explore the Roman countryside in search of water. As I bicycle out along the old Appian Way with my friend Edoardo, we find ourselves, though still well within the administrative confines of the now sprawling capital, in the countryside. It is not, however, quite the soft, rolling hills and sunflowers of Tuscany. Rather it is arid and lush. Thorny brambles, fig trees, and the odd holm oak spring from dry, rocky soil. Here and there are cleared fields with artichokes or *ortaggi (wild greens and vegetables)*. Except for those that built the occasional fence to keep sheep in or out, no hand has constrained this landscape, though many have painted it. Poussin, Fragonard, and countless other artists were drawn to the timeless ruins to be found amid the overgrown vegetation and the local farmers' and shepherds' blithe disrespect for the ruins charmed them even more.

Edoardo, I have found, knows (more or less) where the city's best-kept secrets are hiding, and, sure enough, he is leading me toward one with great conviction, if not absolute certainty. I begin to doubts his powers as he repeatedly mumbles "it's around here somewhere" and doubles back to look more carefully. But then we finally spy it, barely visible below riotous vegetation: a spring, in the form of a sunken, overgrown pool of greenish water, partially enclosed by an apse-shaped indentation in the hillside. I hear the sound of water and see where it springs from the wall, beneath an aged statue of a female figure. Edoardo explains to me that this is the goddess Egeria, one of the female deities Romans believed presided over woodland springs, and that it was made at some point in the late Roman Empire. Had I been better prepared I might have recognized the place from Giovanni Battista Piranesi's 18th-century etching, one of many etchings the great Venetian architect made of the Roman countryside. But this was a spontaneous outing, not a research trip. Later I would learn that the mountain nymph was most often associated with groves of trees and water and that this source of water in particular, a spring that fed into the Almone River, was sacred to early Romans. It was, famously, the only place where the Vestal Virgins could fill their vessels.

It makes sense that Romans would imbue natural resources with godlike qualities, as the Greeks and other civilizations did before them. Deifying precious natural resources—the seas, forests, earth, and sun—had long proven an effective way to prevent pollution or abuse. How better to ensure the purity of water and the integrity of a forest than to appoint a deity as protector?

Today this site is more accessible, maintained within a new public park, the *Parco della Caffarella*. Nearby, on the modern road, stands the Acqua Egeria bottling plant whose logo depicts the overgrown spring under the slogan *"Acqua Santa di Roma,"* Rome's Holy Water. Romans drive out with crates of empty bottles in the back of their Fiats and, for a small fee, fill them with water from stainless steel spigots labeled *frizzante* and *naturale*. They may not know the full story of the ancient nymphs, but they certainly recognize the importance of good water.

Leaving the Parco della Caffarella we head across the no-man's land that is Rome's *periferia* or suburban sprawl, to another nascent urban park which defines the edge between city and countryside: *il Parco degli Acquedotti*. I recently found, in an old sketchbook of mine, a photo-montage I once created to capture a fleeting moment in the park. It was the view, from the Naples-bound train, of the tracks intersecting a double row of Roman pine trees, which in turn scissor through the arcades of the Acqua Claudia aqueduct.

Sketch collage (by author) of Roman aqueducts, pine trees and power lines

Now that I am biking under these vast stone arches of the Roman aqueducts as they march across the Roman countryside towards the distant dome of St. Peter's, I am acutely aware of the web of flows that comprise our cities today. Power lines crisscross as they bring electricity to the city, while gas pipes, modern water pipes and the city sewer system are buried below ground. Overhead, low-flying planes dip toward Rome's Ciampino airport. Trains slide by noisily to and from Termini Station.

Whereas back in the city center we are more aware of the boundaries and access points–the Aurelian Wall and its gates are still for the most part intact–out here we feel that cities are more about flows than they are about fixed structures. Again quoting William Mitchell, "the story of recent urban growth has not been one of successive encircling walls, as it mostly would have been for ancient, medieval and Renaissance cities, but of network-induced sprawl at the fringes." This network-building seems anything but recent as we contemplate the construction of the Acqua Claudia, begun under Caligula and finished by his successor, Claudius, in 50 CE. By this time, ensuring respect for water no longer demanded its personification in deities like Egeria. The power of Rome's engineering and recognition of the human ingenuity it entailed, was more than enough to command reverence and prevent abuse. In both cases a respect for limited resources was built into their delivery system, whether your water gushed forth from a sacred spring or was carried along towering arches into the glorious public fountains.[8]

As we continue our ride across the fields, I learn that Edoardo's familiarity with this area was partly due to his cinema connections. Son of a great *Dolce Vita* era actor, and involved in the dubbing business himself, he spent time on the sets of the big productions in the film studios of Cinecittà, Rome's Hollywood, a stone's throw from the aqueducts. Cinema and Rome's hinterland have often overlapped. It was amidst these very ruins, in the casually chaotic landscape of Rome's expanding hinterland, that Pier Paolo Pasolini shot the most poignant scenes of *Mamma Roma* and his earlier short film *La Ricotta*. A poet and filmmaker from Italy's northern Friuli region, Pasolini was fascinated by the lives of Rome's underclasses, the residents of the borgata (planned fascist-era towns) but also of the unplanned and illegally-built shanty towns at the margins of the capital. In the early 1960s, he directed his camera lens at the squalid but somehow sublime living conditions of the marginalized subproletariat living amongst the ruins of the aqueducts. He was particularly drawn to the Via del Mandrione, sandwiched between the Acqua Claudia and the Acqua Felice, in his time still a squatter settlement inhabited especially by semi-nomadic Rom who made a living as horse-suppliers and extras for the big productions in Cinecitta' nearby. Perhaps like the hydraulic infrastructure, exposed to view instead of hidden discretely in the walls and floors as it would in conventional architecture, the protagonists of Pasolini's films (only rarely played by professional actors) serve to bring to the surface the inner workings of our society, in the words of Saskia Sassen to "make legible the obscure.[9]"

When the source of water is at the edge of town, the architecture of the network is usually quite evident, as in the case of the Acqua Claudia, now squeezed in by building-supply yards, fenced-in spontaneous housing, illegal landfills, and other detritus of contemporary Rome's *periferia*. A resource is transported through a structured channel from the source (exploited to varying degrees) to its end user. Along the way, inefficiencies and waste abound, and profit is extracted.

Also in the Parco degli Aquedotti, for example, I helped others excavate an immense 2nd-century villa that blatantly tapped water from the Acqua Marcia. At least Rome's ancient water system was "transparent." Today we more often consume resources that come from places far from our immediate view. This makes access less of a sure thing, and it is access to clean water "furnished to us gratuitously" as Vitrivius said, that allows our cities to prosper. The amount of water on the planet hasn't changed throughout human history, but the portion available for human use, fresh and non-polluted, is threatened.

Rome's tradition of public access to free water dates to around 25 BCE. As part of a concerted effort by the first Emperor Augustus to secure support through public works, Marcus Agrippa established Rome's first public baths, which were fed by the Acqua Vergine, the city's shortest but also one of its most longevous aqueducts. The Baths of Agrippa were located in the Campus Martius, just behind the Pantheon, which Agrippa also constructed. Like later and larger public baths, Agrippa's complex provided separate chambers for hot, warm and cold water (the *caldarium, tepidarium* and *frigidarium* respectably). It fast became a gathering place for Roman citizens. A generation of American study-abroad students and faculty had the privilege of occupying studio space and classrooms in the remains of the *caldarium*, on Via Arco della Ciambella, the street of the "arch of the donut," where the donut was the domed, cylindrical bathing hall. From the design studio windows we viewed the circular concrete structure into which are still tucked homes and shops from later centuries.

Apart from the actual bathing in water, baths served important roles in what we would today call "wellness." Exercise was fundamental to the baths and a workout usually preceded the rubdown, immersion and rinsing phases. Bodily functions were accepted as part of public daily activities, at least if we are to judge by the scatalogical humor at the "Baths of the Seven Wise Men" at Ostia Antica. But baths also served an important thermal function and will be addressed in the chapter dedicated to energy.

One of Rome's typical Roman *nasone* fountains

Fountains

Ask a visitor to Rome in August what stood out most and the answer will often be the presence of fountains. The list of fountains is long, especially when we include the simple but beautiful *nasoni* drinking fountains, cast-iron cylinders with beak-like, continuously-flowing outlets from which every Roman and most discerning travelers have learned the trick to drink comfortably.

Three of Rome's most spectacular fountains share connections to Gian Lorenzo Bernini. The *Barcaccia* at the foot of the Spanish Steps was designed by Pietro Bernini, father of the more famous Baroque architect and sculptor. In order to preserve the water pressure of its aqueduct for fountains elsewhere, Bernini devised a narrative solution which justified a fountain sunken below street level: a sinking boat (or *barcaccia*) that has taken on water and is overflowing at its sides. On a hot day, descending onto the marble stepping stone at the port or prow end of the boat, you are rewarded simultaneously with a cool mist, a musical sound which drowns out the street noise above, and a drink of delicious cold water.

From this point, the conduits were diverted in the 16th century under what is appropriately called Via Condotti (street of the conduits) and would later supply Gian Lorenzo Bernini's greatest fountain, the Fountain of the Four Rivers a half-mile away in Piazza Navona.

Bernini also had a hand in Rome's most famous fountain, the Trevi, which is also fed by the Acqua Vergine. When he was appointed architect of the aqueduct in 1629, Bernini was asked to design a replacement for a basin that provided water to a neighborhood on the Quirinal Hill just below the papal summer palace. His plan for it was not quite feasible, but a century later it had an enormous influence on Nicolo Salvi, the architect who *did* design Trevi Fountain in 1732. No other fountain in the world celebrates water with such theatricality, nor blurs the lines so expertly between nature and artifice. John Pinto points out that "rather than seeming shaped by the hand of man, the *scogli* appear to have been deeply eroded by the action of the water, which courses through and over them, to create an extraordinarily expressive form of abstract sculpture[10]. Salvi populates his faux natural landscape with stone flora and fauna, from prickly pairs to a snail crawling on a marsh marigold. Here, like experiments in biomimicry coming out of cutting-edge architecture schools, art is made to imitate nature, but unlike contemporary reliance on computers and para-metrics, in the 17th century the critical eye and hand of the artist was required. Salvi "often climbed out onto the *scogli* (rocks) with charcoal stick in hand to sketch particular details on the surface of the travertine." And the work only succeeds because of the dialogue it sparks with the spectator.

The Acqua Vergine has its source ten kilometers outside the city, a spring discovered, according to the legend, by a young woman after whom the pure "virgin" water was named. After Caligula demolished much of it because it blocked the amphitheatre he was constructing, Claudius rebuilt it and it is Claudius' name we see carved in the monumental arch at Via Nazzareno where the aqueduct spanned a road. Unlike most aqueducts, it has never ceased to carry water for the simple reason that outside the center it is underground and resistant to destruction. In 1937 the Vergine Nuova was built along the same route but in a separate channel to augment its flow.

The Vergine is really more of a drain than an aqueduct, with feeder pipes entering it. Not far from the here it morphs into a sewer, carrying its bounty of water out towards the Tiber while collecting ever more water from street level drains. The drain under the oculus of the Pantheon, for example, feeds into this extension of the Vergine according to the thick blue line on Rodolfo Lanciani's map, the Forma Urbis. In the Middle Ages, the Frangipani family controlled the ancient aqueduct with a fortress, determining who had access to the water at what price.

To understand more fully water's role in this part of Rome,

turn your back to the Trevi fountain, duck around the first street after the church, and descend into the archaeological excavation almost ten meters below modern street level. In the early 2000s, food-services mega-company Gruppo Cremonini restored the building, creating a bookstore, restaurant, underground (literally) cinema and a publicly-accessible archaeological site. The site goes by several names, Cinema Trevi, or Vicus Caprarius (goat alley, after a place of animal sacrifice that may once have stood on the ancient street) or Città dell'Acqua (city of water). The site contains several structures, including a tenement house from the 2nd century CE (that was transformed into an upscale mansion in the 5th century) and a cistern which in the Middle Ages, after most aqueducts had been cut, stored 150,000 liters of this valuable liquid commodity in two cement lined rooms. Water is still present at the lowest level, close to the city's water table, dripping through the walls and sitting transparently in shallow pools over ancient paving tiles.

Back on the surface, looking at the Trevi Fountain gushing water in all its splendor, it is common to hear snide remarks about Rome's modern plumbing. Everyone who has spent time in Rome has hydraulic anecdotes to tell, usually involving lack of water pressure or cold showers. The days of imperial aqueducts and public thermal baths are long over, but water is still very present in Roman life. The apartment we moved to after getting married, near Termini station, had three water faucets in the kitchen. I learned that the extra one was for *acqua diretta*, though not as abundant, it was fresh and pure as opposed to the normal hot and cold which carried *acqua di cassoni* through a rooftop cistern and thus could get contaminated. We would use the *acqua diretta* for drinking and other uses for which purity was essential, but had no qualms about washing and flushing toilets with *acqua di cassoni*. To many this separate system was an embarrassing holdover from the wartime year's of depravation and couldn't wait for the cisterns to be phased out. But I actually saw it as a smart choice, a means of calibrating our domestic habits to optimize performance. Like pulling the shutters closed to keep out the sun, having choices makes us more free. Watering our plants, filling our pools and flushing away our waste in clean drinking water is not a sign of progress.

Today Rome's water supply, though only half what it was in antiquity per capita, is still one of the most abundant in the world, making Rome the only European capital whose water resources are recharged faster than the city can drain them. Amidst all this abundance, it pains us to remember that 780 million people live without clean drinking water[11].

So aren't Rome's constantly flowing fountains somehow contributing to planetary water shortage? To understand why the answer is no, we have to go to the source of the water. Typical of most of the aqueducts, although the longest and most capacious, is the Aqua Marcia which begins its 90 kilometer journey to Rome in the upper Anio river basin at a place called Agosta. Here numerous springs fed into catchment channels which, in turn, fed the main channel of the aqueduct which was completed by Roman praeto Q. Marcius Rex in 140 BCE. This water streams constantly from the ground, especially plentiful in the springtime when the snow on the Apennines melts, but adequate year round to feed Rome's fountains. Even if never funneled into artificial pipes, it would still travel more or less the same route on its way to the sea; the Romans simply (!) detoured it through their baths, fountains, latrines and drains and if these were all shut off at once the pressure at the source would have caused other channels to form. Rather than simply conserving water in a city blessed with its abundance, the challenge is to devise ways of sending this water to places that suffer from drought, such as Puglia and Calabria. Or perhaps better, finding ways in which more people can benefit from this supply of fresh water without taxing other limited resources such as land and energy. As clean water re-emerges as it was in antiquity as the limiting planetary resource of the 21st century (the "new oil" according to some), Rome may discover ways to leverage its water supplies as generators for growth.

In 2011 Rome held a referendum to decide whether its water supply should remain public or become privatized. The question was not as simple as the posters showing coin-operated water fountains would have you think; all services have to some extent come under private management in recent years in an attempt to improve efficiency and reduce the bloated public sector. But what was at play was the very life-blood of humanity here and for it to become a corporate commodity was worth questioning. It was not surprising that people voted overwhelmingly to keep water public since access to water has always been at the base of political support. At the time of Frontinus, water was a public resource, distributed for free in public baths and fountains but also for a fee through concessions to private entrepreneurs whose baths were more exclusive and provided other perks. Water itself was a *bene comune,* a public asset, like the food distribution and the entertainment at the Colosseum (the proverbial "bread and circuses"). Free, clean water was one of the rewards for being Roman. In the event of a shortage of water due to a faulty aqueduct or damaged cistern, the private concessionaires would be the first to forfeit their supply, and the public drinking water the last to be shut off.

Today one hears about "smart city" solutions, soft technologies that work with natural forces rather than against them. In an age of impending climate crisis, cities with longstanding experience in limiting and adapting to floods (Amsterdam and Venice to name a few) are well positioned to lead the battle to survive rising sea levels. In the same way Rome, with its millennia-long hydraulic know-how, might spearhead the global drive for smart water management. And that's something to drink to.

Notes

1. John Hopkins, "The Cloaca Maxima and the Monumental Manipulation of Water in Archaic Rome," in *Waters of Rome, Number 4, March 2007,* posted on http://www3.iath.virginia.edu/waters/Journal4Hopkins.pdf, 8.

2. Lewis Mumford, *The City in History*, (New York: Harcourt, Brace and World. 1961).

3. Paul Bennett, "Rome's Ruins" in *National Geographic*, July 2006

4. William Mitchell, *Me++ The Cyborg Self and the Networked City.* (Cambridge, MA: MIT Press, 2004)

5. This previously forgotten aspect of architecture was the subject of Reyner Banham's 1969 book Architecture of the Well-Tempered Environment.

6. "Garibaldi and the Improvement of the Capital." The New York Times 7 Mar. 1875

7. For more on this see Heiken, Grant, et. al. *The Seven Hills of Rome: a Geological Tour of the Eternal City.* (Princeton: Princeton University Press. 2005)

8. Later I will bring travel personality Rick Steves to this site; the documentary we end up making will put this place on the map for

international tourists, helping them once again to become a destination for the new Grand Tour.

9. Saskia Sassen, "Seeing Like a City" in Burdett, Ricky, ed. *The Endless City*. (London: Phaidon. 2007).

10. John A Pinto, *The Trevi Fountain*. (New Haven and London: Yale University Press, 1986), 150.

11. https://www.foodandwaterwatch.org/water/interesting-water-facts/

CHAPTER 2.

GREEN SPACE: EUROPE'S GREENEST

"Oggi abbiamo delle cime di rapa appena arrivate." Your waiter in the small trattoria near Campo de' Fiori will switch to passable English if necessary, but not by default. An older man who has probably worked in the same family-run restaurant all his life, he has short white hair and wears a tight white vest over a white shirt and black trousers. He is telling you that they

have just received a crate of *cime di rapa*, a kind of broccoli flower, and this comes as a tacit recommendation to order seasonal and local. If you have a reasonable, special request, a simple red sauce or a green salad, the kitchen will usually be happy to fulfill it even if it's not on the menu, but beware that if you ask for artichokes in June or peaches in October your waiter will not conceal his disdain. His expertise is food, not communication. If asked, he is happy to explain the subtle differences between *cicoria* and *biedina* and other cooked greens. He will tell you how they are best served and he will know exactly where and when they were harvested or gathered.

If the *trattoria* serves meat, you will be offered a limited range of cuts chosen by the trusted butcher off of the carcass you may have seen hauled off a truck double-parked outside his shop nearby earlier in the day.

If instead you are in the mood for seafood it's likely that a cart will be wheeled out for you on which a small array of shiny fish glisten in the sun. This is not an illustration of the types of fish they have, like photographs of menu items to facilitate ordering. These are the *actual* fish they have today; pick one and they will send it back to the kitchen to be cooked. The fish is almost certainly from yesterday's Mediterranean catch, just as the steak was cut from animals slaughtered a few days earlier, and the fruit and vegetables are seasonal and local.

Kilometro Zero

Most of what is brought to your table originated within 100 kilometers. Ironically, the product likely to have travelled the farthest is the one we have already seen to be abundant locally: water. Depending on your response to the question *frizzante o naturale*, sparkling or still, you may be brought *Ferrarelle*, from around Naples or *Levissima* from the Alps, or any of hundreds of other brands of bottled water. It is possible, though by no means common, that you will be served *Egeria*, Rome's *Acqua Santa*, which has started adding the words "0 Km" to its label. Less likely still, you might be offered simple tap water. Although it is clean and tasty, it is a bit too heavy in calcium for many, and more importantly, it cannot be used to inflate the check. New restaurants, like Porto Fluviale in the Ostiense quarter, have started offering their own bottled water, purified in house and served in their own branded bottles.

You are eating lunch in the heart of Rome, in a building that has stood here for centuries and probably housed a variety of functions before being converted to its current use. If you are a visitor to Rome, chances are you arrived on foot from nearby and will be walking or taking public transit or a cab to your next destination. But you might be surprised at how many "locals" eating at nearby tables actually came by car, leaving tons of steel blocking the alleys nearby. And at other hours, delivery vans clog the same narrow streets. You can still encounter hand carts wheeling crates of fruit through busy streets, or a butcher negotiating a corner with a side of beef slung over his shoulder (or, for that matter, a gallery owner hauling an 18th century landscape painting or contemporary bronze sculpture.) Unlike Venice, though, where deliveries can only make the last few hundred meters from water by foot, Rome relies heavily on motorized vehicles to get food to the table. They may be tiny three wheeled *Api* vans, or even *Vespas* with crates precariously strapped to the back, but they add to the noise, emissions and general hazards nevertheless. In her book *Hungry City*, architect Carolyn Steele points out how amazing it is that cities are even capable of taking care of the complex task of feeding millions of residents and visitors every day.

In Rome the consequences of getting our food, ourselves and our waste in and out of the dense historical center are visibly amplified. Rare are the restaurants with back doors for delivery, never mind loading docks. Everything, and everyone, usually comes in and out through one front door. This is another case of "making visible the obscure," and one that makes it easy–at least for those of us who spend a lot of time prowling Rome at all hours–to judge food quality without even asking for a menu. The frozen food truck parked on the sidewalk is worse negative advertising than any scathing reviews on Trip Advisor. And empty cardboard cartons from food multinationals, piled amongst empty water bottles waiting for trash pickup, speak poorly for both the environmental commitment and gastronomic quality of the restaurant that dumped them.

If the topic of green brings to mind parks and gardens, you may be surprised that discussions of green space in Italy often return to the subject of food. (True, this could be said of discussions of *anything* in Italy, but green and food are particularly connected). In Italy food is still grounded in place and time. It is local and seasonal. On the one hand, choice is limited; you won't find fresh tomatoes in December. On the other hand, when tomatoes are in season you can choose between dozens of varieties and, within them, from infinite exemplars. Each peach is unique, not selected (or engineered!) to meet restrictive "ideal" standards of size, shape, and appearance. Variety is, of course, not a value in itself–think of the hundreds of TV channels with nothing worth watching. No, variety means little unless it provides value. Usually, in nature, variety (let's call it bio-diversity) exists for a reason and it is to make an ecosystem more resilient and capable of adaptation. By editing variety out of our produce in the name of standardization we have boxed ourselves into a particularly grim corner.

Whereas industrial systems rely on power, regenerative systems rely on information. Wes Jackson argues that we are experiencing not a boom in information but an impoverishment, in that species are being lost at an alarming rate, and biodiversity equals information[1]. In fact, the demise of multifarious biological species, to be replaced by monoculture farming parallels the globalization of culture, with the elimination of dialects, craftskills and literary or artistic diversity. About 6,000 different languages are spoken around the world. But the Foundation for Endangered Languages estimates that every year the world loses around 25 mother tongues. Likewise, genetic engineering, far from synthesizing new species is working to eliminate natural complexity and reduce species to a small, manageable number.

Food is not just limited in time; it is also limited to a reasonable distance from its place of production. This is not to say we can't get any food anywhere; it's just a question of cost and impact. Proximity has clear benefits when it comes to food, the most obvious being that the closer food is to its final destination the fresher it is on arrival. It is estimated that 40% of the ecological footprint of today's cities is tied to food, much of this not in the production and processing phases but afterwards, in delivery, refrigeration, preparation and disposal. Much of Rome's produce comes from within the city limits themselves. Without leaving the confines of the city it is common to see sheep grazing, dairy cattle, vegetable crops and even vineyards. This is partly because the administrative boundaries of Rome contain over 1,200 square kilometers, drawn far beyond the settled zone of the city at the time of Italy's unification in preparation for eventual expansion. But it is also a question of culture. Romans recognize that without accessible, productive agricultural land, much of what makes cities thrive would be impossible.

Artichokes at the Campagna Amica Farmer's Market

Slow down, Food

Italy, thankfully, is behind the times when it comes to dumbing down food, but it has been moving in this direction nevertheless. Here, as elsewhere in the developed world, food provision has moved from small shops to supermarket chains in recent decades and multi-national fast food chains have started to make inroads into the country, after perhaps France, most associated with local gastronomic traditions. In the mid-eighties, in reaction and resistance to this trend, Carlo Petrini, an Italian food writer from Piedmont, launched the Slow Food movement. The occasion was a very specific (and symbolic) grassroots campaign to keep McDonalds out of Rome. Although the campaign failed–McDonalds' first location at the Spanish Steps was followed by hundreds more throughout the country–Petrini astutely exploited the inevitable media spotlight that big brands attracted and diffused it across the rich terrain of Italian food culture. He turned a critique into a commodity, and a successful one at that, with some 800 local chapters and members in 150 countries. Food, whether fast or slow, is still business.

Most of my *gastrofighetti* friends ("foodies" sounds better in Italian) will agree that while Rome is still a great city for people who eat, of late it has been easier to pay excessively to eat mediocre food. On the one hand this is the fault of a not-always-informed public that succumbs to the attraction of a good location and deceptive marketing; the checked tablecloths and chianti flask will cajole a surprising number of tourists. But there has also been a disturbing infiltration of organized crime into the food business, exemplified by the purchase of notable restaurants and cafes by shell companies belonging to known criminal families. [2] Roberto Saviano, journalist and author of Gomorrah, in a recent article on what he terms "Camorra Food Inc." describes how almost every branch of the food business in Italy (and not only) has been infiltrated by criminal organizations. "Our every action," he writes, "from the first thing we do in the morning through dinner, can enrich the clan unbeknownst to us.[3]"

Even when there are no insinuations of wrongdoings, the arrival of big food in Rome is disconcerting. I recently attended the inauguration of the giant high-end food emporium Eataly in Rome's Ostiense neighborhood, a vibrant but marginalized urban area that is already a magnet for foodies. Food Blogger Katie Parla[4] describes Eataly as resembling "an upscale food court at an American mall," and in answer to the obvious question why, quotes Nicola Farinetti, son of the chain's founder: "Unfortunately the world of small food shops, those small places dedicated to quality food, like Americans imagine, died many years ago."

Thankfully, this is not entirely true although, if it were, what irony to think that those same Americans who have introduced the world to one-stop shopping are now waxing nostalgic for a more diversified food market that this "optimized" distribution has supplanted. Nearby in Testaccio, the traditional daily produce market has recently been relocated to a new structure but is still thriving, as is a weekend farmers' market set up in a repurposed industrial space nearby. Even with its through-the-roof prices, high-end food boutique Volpetti is going strong. And the *Città dell'Altra Economia*, which has struggled to promote fair trade, organic farming and other sustainable practices, is still striving to continue activities in the former slaughterhouse (which itself gave rise in the 20th century to many of Rome's famous meat dishes).

Most Americans I know in Rome are un-enthusiastic about Eataly. They are far more inspired by the Rome Sustainable Food Project at the American Academy in Rome. Launched by writer and restauranteur Alice Waters and chef Mona Talbott with the aim to construct a replicable model for sustainable dining in an institution, the project develops relationships with local farmers and provenders as well as growing almost all of its own produce. Few passersby on the quiet street on the Janiculum Hill know that behind the facade of the grand beaux-arts palace, designed a hundred years ago by American architects McKim, Meade and White, kitchen staff and volunteers are busy cultivating a vibrant and productive garden. Dining in the Academy courtyard recently opposite architect Carolyn Steele, an expert on eating and urbanism, we discussed the changing role food is finding in cities. Thanks to Slow Food and a vast and viral range of food-related ventures, citizens are starting to ask where their food comes from. And they want to know more about the people or corporations responsible for it. Some people may be fooled by checkered table-cloths out front and ignore the frozen food trucks out back, but more and more frequently people want to look in the kitchen and hear the true stories behind the bounty on the dinner table.

Roman Locavores

The global food industry is not new. When Rome's population exceeded one million it was at the center of a vast food network; the Mediterranean rim provided grain, oil (olive, that is), wine, citrus and other fruits while the sea itself was tapped for fish. Salt and spices often came from distant shores.

Born of agriculture (Romulus, legend has it, plowed a furrow to define the boundaries of Roma Quadrata), Rome long maintained a reverence for its humble farming origins. Temples to Saturn and Ceres (Agriculture and Grain) were especially venerated. Sacred plants, the olive, fig and grape, were cultivated in the Forum (where they can still be seen today thanks to 20th century replanting). Cicero wrote that "of all the occupations by which gain is secured, none is better than agriculture, none more profitable, none more delightful, none more becoming to a free man." Pliny the Elder wrote extensively about agriculture in his *Naturalis Historia* and the 2nd century BCE writer Cato dedicated a whole treatise to farming, considering it not just necessary but noble. Land ownership was among the most respected sources and symbols of wealth in Republican-era Italy. Farmland was awarded to returning soldiers as a prize for heroic actions on the battlefield, and family farms were amassed through strategic marriages. The city of Rome grew surrounded by productive farmland. Anthony Majanlahti's book *The Fam-*

ilies That Made Rome describes how power for much of the city's history has meant land[5]. Mergers, marriages, acquisitions and the likes led to larger and larger estates, and since land is limited, part of this expansion required the privatization of what had been held in common. And land speculation was not only a local affair.

By the height of Rome's imperial power, agriculture had become a global enterprise. Ships arrived from Africa at the port near Ostia at the mouth of the Tiber carrying amphora filled with grain, olive oil, sardines (whole and processed), salted mackerel, and a fermented fish sauce known as *garum*. A stone relief found in Ostia (now in the Vatican Museums) depicts men unloading bags of grain and barrels (of wine?) from a ship. Although Egypt was called Rome's breadbasket, wheat might come from Sicily, Sardinia, Spain or almost anywhere else in the region. Apparently, even India and China were in on the outsourcing, as testified by Roman finds in Arikamedu and accounts of ancient Roman ambassadors in both Indian and Chinese writings.

Since shipping cost significantly less by sea than by land — 1/60th according to some estimates —, boat building was a big industry. So big, in fact, that by the 2nd century trees for masts were so scarce they had to be imported from the Dalmatian coast, and later from England. Central Italy had been for all extents and purposes deforested. Clive Ponting, in *Green History of the World*, describes the destruction of Tuscany's beach and elm forests, sacrificed for fuel and construction timber. In order to import food from distant sources, it became necessary to import other materials and slaves from distant sources, which in turn led to the need of more ships and labor to propel them, a vicious circle indeed. In fact, like any unsustainable system, Roman trade imploded.

By the 5th century it was no longer feasible to transport food across great distances, but neither was such long-distance agriculture necessary to feed Rome. From over a million the city's population had dropped to less than 50,000. With so few inhabitants, large tracts of urban land were abandoned, becoming what would later become known as the *disabitato* or uninhabited land. No longer needed to shelter the masses, these empty lots were either left to nature (and grazing animals) or planted with orchards, vineyards and garden vegetables. According to Richard Krautheimer, by the 15th century the city could be divided into *abitato*, the inhabited section mostly near the river, and the vast ares of *disabitato*. A visitor to Rome in the Renaissance would find a cow pasture in the place of the old Roman Forum. The Imperial palaces on the Palatine Hill had crumbled and become overgrown with vineyards. Over half of the city was now uninhabited, used in most cases for orchards and gardens.

The presence of predominantly spontaneous green space from the Renaissance onwards is well-illustrated in the city plan exquisitely surveyed and drawn by GiovanBattista Nolli. In the heart of the ancient city, where the Roman Forum once stood, Nolli writes *Campo Vaccino*, or field of cows, and along the Via Sacra where the triumphal processions once marched he draws a simple line of trees. Everywhere on this map the words *vigna* (vineyard), *villa* and *orte* (garden) paint a picture of a surprisingly green city. Jim Tice of the University of Oregon writes "Nolli's rendering seems to prove that the urban center had a vital and complementary hinterland that not only served as a retreat for its wealthy families and ecclesiastics but one that presumably served as its bread basket."[6] The walls of Rome no longer separated urban from extra-urban but allowed for both urban fabric and productive green space to coexistence within their perimeter.

It might be said that the city was healthier than it had ever been. According to Charles Waldheim, in the *disabitato* we can find "agrarian models for contemporary urbanism.[7]" More and more, architects today are turning to landscape as a laboratory for sustainable cities and Italy provides rich precedents.

In the medieval city of Siena, in the heart of Tuscany, a similar situation to 18th century Rome is strikingly evident, perhaps more so because of the smaller scale of the city and its limited development in more recent times. Looking out from the *loggia*, the great covered terrace, of the *Palazzo Pubblico*, you note the red brick walls of the city that sweep out across the rolling hills, dividing verdant farmland from (more) verdant farmland. In the early 14th century Siena was on a steep growth curve, battling neighboring Florence for status as Tuscan stronghold. Construction began on its massive cathedral enlargement and new city walls were made ready to embrace an expanding population. Then in 1348 the plague hit. Siena lost 30-50 percent of its population and never rebounded. The church was left unfinished as it still stands today and the city would never again grow to reach its new walls.

One of the people who died in Siena that year was Ambrogio Lorenzetti, the painter who ten years earlier had frescoed the walls of the Council Room in the the *Palazzo Pubblico*. Entitled *The Allegory of Good and Bad Government* the paintings depict the city in various guises, from virtuous to villainous. What they have in common, apart from the clustered palaces, markets, towers, churches, streets and walls in varying states of disrepair is the presence, beyond the walls, of agricultural land. For Lorenzetti a city cannot exist without the country; they are bound together in inevitable unbreakable whole, a fact which dominated cities of the past. While it is the rare city today that has not broken this bond to its neighboring countryside, Siena, thanks to its abrupt downturn in the 14th century, has preserved it. Today, after viewing Lorenzetti's paintings, and then climbing to to the loggia to view both heart of the city and its surrounding bucolic landscape, you can descend into the orchards and cultivated fields of the *Orti Pecci* a five minute walk away. Here you see residents harvest the crops which will grace their tables at dinnertime.

Land and its Limits

The example of Siena — and really any medieval town — is of the establishment of city limits and a clear, black-and-white relationship between city and country. Most often this has meant creating a city where there was only land. Vitruvius describes the first steps in choosing a healthy site, laying out the city grid and defining its limits, the future walls, roads and gates. But the history of urbanization has often been the creation of land out of "nothing." Venice as we know it was created in a lagoon on 117 islands. Amsterdam is still creating land on which to concentrate new expansion, such as the Borneo Sporenberg residential project or Zeeberg. Dubai's Palm Island is the most recent and spectacular example, and one of the least sustainable.

Land could also be fabricated where there was none by draining swamps, through land reclamation projects such as the Pontine mashes, where in the Renaissance the Medici launched an ambitious but eventually unsuccessful project to drain the swamps and claim as theirs any dry land thus created. In 1922 the Fascist government launched the "battle of the swamps" which would be fought principally by immigrants from the Veneto and Friuili regions, who were called upon for their experience with canal construction and management. The strategy was comprised of three phases: land reclamation, agricultural settlement and malaria elimination. Today the Pontine Marshes are marshes no more, but the canals and much of the agricultural land created out of thin air (or rather murky water) is now threatened by the impact of urbanization. The population of the Pontine marshes has gone from under a thousand residents in the 1920s to over half a million today, and the provincial capital of Latina (founded from scratch as the fascist new town of Littoria in 1932) is second in size only to Rome in the Lazio region. To address the problem of environmental pollution, the Province of Latina recently signed an agreement with M.I.T.'s Project for Reclamation Excellence to design a master ecological plan for the most polluting part of this region. Landscape architect Alan Berger, who launched the project while at the American Academy in Rome, talks of the creation of an artificial nature. "We are trying to invent an ecosystem in the midst of an entirely engineered, polluted landscape,[8]" he says. Almost a century after the creation of new towns in former swamps, entropy has resulted in a vague blend of urban and rural, quite the opposite of the clear limits depicted in Lorenzetti's painting. Berger's team is working to engineer a new, artificial wetland to do the job of filtering pollutants that nature has always done.

Globally, we see simultaneous trends of deforestation to create agricultural land and, elsewhere, the conversion of agricultural lands to "urban" use. In Europe, 2 percent of agricultural land is lost to development every ten years. 60 percent of earth's land surface was once forested; now less than half of that remains, a condition that leads to massive erosion and drought. About 11 percent of the global landscape is now cropland. Deforestation is not a new phenomena, although its rapidity and scale has escalated aggressively.

In ancient Rome, the landscape was viewed as something to

dominate and then replicate with precision. Barbara A. Kellum writes of the first emperor Augustus as "well aware of the evocative nature of plants and trees...famed for choosing to decorate his own villas, not so much with handsome statues and pictures as with terraces and groves." Evidence of Plato's student Theophrastus shows that deforestation was already a problem in the Greek world, bringing a combination of drought and flooding. According to writings by Pliny the Elder, flooding of the Tiber was a problem in the first century CE, and his nephew Pliny the Younger describes the high-water table at the family villa near Rome. Although there is no conclusive evidence linking these hydrological problems to deforestation, we know that they are paralleled by a massive clearing of forests for agricultural land, lumber and fuel. And though deforestation declines along with population in the middle ages, by 1500 Europeans were again consuming one ton of wood/person/year. Only at the turn of the new millennium, as part of the UN millennium development goals, has the direction shifted.

Ironically, in Rome itself, in this very moment when the world is rediscovering the importance of biodiversity, of local food production, and of green zones as essential to human inhabitation, the green "capitol" of Italy's green capital is disappearing like rain forests in Brazil. A more local, though more anachronistic, analogy that comes to mind is the destruction of antiquities in Renaissance Rome, usually carried out by exactly those humanist patrons who claimed a renewed enthusiasm for antiquities; in a similar manner the speculative growth currently consuming the *campagna romana* is often promoted as "green." Today more and more streets are paved over and, worse, large tracts of former farmland become "urbanized" with residential enclaves claiming to provide the best of both worlds, access to city conveniences while immersed in a green context. I often question why we use the term "urbanization" to refer to turning land which can produce food for a dense, adjacent population at minimum energy cost into toxic structures which may never be inhabited and, if they are, will require huge expenditures in energy to do so. Perhaps, instead, the maintenance of productive green land, gardens, orchards and grazing land, in close proximity to dense, pedestrian-friendly streets is far more urban than the construction of low-density, single-function buildings.

The disabitato in Campo Vaccino as drawn by Piranesi, circa 1750

The Picturesque Landscape

At the same time land was turning into pure commodity, artists and writers began transforming its image into art, giving birth to a new aesthetic of pastoral beauty: the picturesque landscape. Painters like Poussin, Salvator Rosa and Claude Lorrain made images of fictional rural scenes which inspired landowners to make them real, but on purely visual terms. Any sense of the multifaceted ecosystem was enslaved to the tyranny of the picture. True, in order to allow a natural looking landscape to take form some landscape designers such as the 18th century Englishman Capability Brown adopted a rudimentary understanding of ecology with native plants and controlled wetlands, but it was a far cry from sustainable land management.

Rome's countryside fuels this passion for the romantic landscape, in this case introducing another component: the ruin. The traveller on his or her grand tour has long described, sketched, painted and photographed scenes of a sublime landscape littered with the remains of ancient villas, tombs and other monuments to Rome's greatness. The famous portrait of "Goethe in the Roman Campagna" by Johann Tischbein shows the German writer in a classical pose, but the landscape beyond is the same you would see in Paul Bril's "Capriccio" a century earlier, or Thomas Cole's dramatic landscape a century later. The Roman countryside is timeless in its decay, and will inspire landscapes around the world but especially find its way into the romantic English gardens of William Kent, Humphry Repton and "Capability" Brown himself.

Similarly, this less formal English garden design will infect Europe, showing up in Rome's Villa Borghese which Scottish landscape painter Jacob More redesigned in the late 18th century. While walking through this great park, a tourist on her way to see Bernini statues and Caravaggio paintings at one of the world's most beautiful small house museums might stop a passerby to ask "where is the Villa Borghese?" To which the answer, uttered with amusement or exasperation, is "you are in it, Madam." In fact, the Italian term *villa* refers to the estate, not the buildings on it, a linguistic fact which sheds light on the Italian understanding of the connection between the built and the green environments. Here, in the Piazza di Siena where horses are still trotted around regularly, or in the nearby valley of the deer where the animals are no longer hunted, we understand the inspiration of Frederick Law Olmsted in his design of New York's Central Park, and of Clarke and Rapuano, the architects who brought Roman landscape to New York during the New Deal.

Camillo Sitte, writing in 1901, two years before the death of Olmsted, called parks "the lungs of the city." That same year Ebenezer Howard wrote *Garden Cities of Tomorrow* and, in Italy, architect Rodolfo Lanciani would publish his famous archeological map of Rome, the Forma Urbis. Another architect, Giacomo Boni, was at the same time busy excavating what would become one of the world's densest archaeological parks, the Roman Forum. In London, observing the biological growth of the city, Patrick Geddes invented the science of ecological urbanism as we know it. Although it would be Tansley, in 1935, who first used the term Ecosystem, Geddes envisioned the end of the Paleotecnic age (the age of petroleum) to be replaced by a sustainable Neotecnic age. From Italy to England, the early 19th century saw a rethinking of cities and their landscapes, from archaeology to ecology.

Unlike the archaeologists "unburying" Rome, American environmentalists were until recently still fixated with "greening" everything, mistaking nature for wilderness. This may be because there was still wilderness worth saving when early environmentalists like Emerson and Thoreau wrote. As any scout knows, by living in nature, even with the best intentions, we risk damaging it; even Thoreau once famously burned down a hundred and fifty acres of forest by accident.

In Europe, where the modern environmental movement was

born when there was no undisturbed nature left, the focus is less on preserving and more on integrating human culture with the rest of the natural world. As a species we thrive on nature as the exception to the rule, not as our natural condition. As Andres Duany and other new urbanists are quick to point out, given a choice, people walk less in green areas than in urban ones–there's simply less to attract you there. Instead, a balanced blend of biodiversity and social diversity, or nature and culture, result in a more desirable habitat for humans.

Europe's Greenest Capital

Between farmland, villas and archaeological areas Rome has more green space per capita than any other European capital: 222 square meters compared to Paris' fourteen square meters. Some of this is private gardens, and there are a few large parks such as the Borghese and Doria Pamphilj "villas." A large portion is farmland, although this is being urbanized at a rate of seven square meters a second, a number constantly on the rise (15,000 hectares of Agro Romano are threatened with destruction)[9]. Illegal building in protected archaeological areas takes place undisturbed. Even the parks become "urbanized," invaded by concessions, commerce, "temporary" constructions in the name of recreation and profit and often removed effectively from the public domain[10]. But despite these incursions of the city into its green space, Rome remains a potentially model green city.

In large part this is thanks to the resilience of nature. Tenacious and pervasive, it sometimes just takes over, creeping up the walls of *palazzi* or dripping from the parapets of *terrazze*. In addition to visual beauty this seasonal vegetation on buildings can go a long way in protecting surfaces from direct sunlight which would otherwise gradually traverse masonry walls and radiate heat to interior rooms. And since many creeping plants either drop their leaves or can be seriously pruned back in the winter, the walls tend to be exposed to the sun when the warmth is desired.

Rome's climate is a blessing for plant life. It rarely freezes and long dry spells, though they happen, rarely dry out the ground that has been dampened by long rainy winters and underground streams. Between the grey basalt cobblestone of most city streets, green is wont to grow when left un-trampled.

Urban Agriculture

Beyond the psychological comfort and energy performance, Rome's green space continues to provide exactly what was discussed at the top of the chapter: food. Already containing more farmland than most cities within its boundaries, and boasting a high sense of local food tradition, Rome is well-positioned as a model for inner-city farming. This doesn't result automatically in a sustainable city, of course. According to Ian McHarg, "farming is another kind of mining, dissipating the substances of aeons of summers." But the re-emergence of urban agriculture, in diminution since the mid-twentieth century, is a sign of positive change.

Urban agriculture doesn't bring the country to the city but finds urban synergies that allow for production of the food needed close to the people who need it. In addition to drastically reducing the energy and emissions costs of food transport and ensuring greater freshness, the presence of green space in our cities has direct environmental, social, economic and psychological benefits.

When we talk about urban agriculture it is not about interspersing acres of farmland between apartment buildings, a strategy which would would negate the density and intensity of cities. While there may be a place for large, shared plots in either central parks or in perimeter green belts, an even greater potential lies in the insertion of gardens throughout the city, on rooftops, terraces, in the leftover spaces between infrastructure and urban fabric, and even in the vertical shells of multistory buildings.

A truly green future for Rome will not be based on new "green" real-estate speculation or new "green" parking structures for new "green" automobiles. It must, as a bare minimum, demand, as does London, that any new development be transit oriented, but far better would be a moratorium on the sub-urban conversion of rural land. Then the process of urbanization in the true sense–smart, cradle-to-cradle, resource-based, pedestrian-oriented, bottom-up, zero-emissions, eternally-contemporary city-making, can carry on.

The long but now accelerating process of destruction of the Roman countryside dates back to the establishment of Roma Capitale in 1870 (Rome as capital of Italy, but capital also in the sense of "wealth in the form of money or other assets"), the result of a long battle fought in the name of "republican" ideals against clerical and noble special interests. In 1870, the royalist and capitalist interests prevailed and the breach in the walls of Rome opened on September 20 of that year let into the city a wave of speculative development which would deface and deform the fabric which had taken two millennia to evolve, and seen some of the most sophisticated urban designs, from the proto-modern metropolis of the Roman Empire to the dynamically dispersed city of the Baroque Era. In the place of either an idea or a design for the city, master plans were enacted and subsequently ignored, easily bypassed by variants and loopholes. Year after year, with increasing frequency under the city's former "progressive" left-wing mayor (progress = neo-liberal modernization of real estate speculation) and the city's former "conservative" mayor (conserving the interests of Rome's rich and powerful), large tracts of rural land guilty of falling within the city limits are condemned to a future of cement and automobiles.

Pine forest in Rome's largest public park, Villa Doria Pamphilj

The Third Landscape

French landscape architect Gilles Clémente describes a "third landscape" of urban or rural sites left behind (*délaissé*): "transitional spaces, neglected land (*friches*), swamps, moors, peat bogs, but also roadsides, shores, railroad embankments, etc. …inaccessible places, mountain summits, non-cultivatable areas, deserts; institutional reserves: national parks, regional parks, nature reserves." On the fringes of Rome, remnants of discarded civilization have long provided ripe ground for grass-roots, bottom-up urbanization, spontaneous reuse of unused "blight" areas by the city's sub-proletariat, a truly Roman phenomenon recognized by Pasolini among others. As elsewhere in the developing world, the forces of speculation have been quick to suppress any real city-forming tendency in the name of urban renewal, but the territory, like nature, shows its resilience.

In Rome there is a third kind of green space, one particular to the eternal city, in which history persists in the form of archaeological ruins. From the Palatine Hill or the Roman Forum in the heart of the city, to the surviving swathe of undeveloped land in the *Campagna Romana*, the Park of the Appian Way, these spaces are neither nature nor artifice but a hybrid of the two. The presence of archaeology keeps building at bay and allows for green to thrive, while the controlled presence of non-invasive species transforms the dry, funereal archaeological landscape into a green-scape which enriches the surrounding city. Here amidst the ruins edible plants thrive: olives, grapes, cherries, citrus fruits, wild greens and berries, and Rome's ever-present umbrella pines that produce abundant pine nuts.

Luigi Canina, appointed Commissioner of Antiquities for Rome in 1839, must have anticipated this synergy when he decreed that the Appian Way, the so-called *Regina Viarum*, be protected as a park dedicated to archaeology. Walking along the Appian Way, well within the city limits, it is still possible to find the road blocked by a herd of sheep. They are grazing in the archaeological park under the watch of their shepherd, keeping the grass trimmed around the ancient tombs as they have done for millennia. Their milk is used at the nearby farmhouse knowns as the Casale della Vaccareccia to produce fresh ricotta cheese that you may well be served at your trattoria in the heart of the city a few miles away.

Notes

1. Wes Jackson, *Consulting the Genius of the Place: An Ecological Approach to a New Agriculture* (Los Angeles: Counterpoint Books, 2010)

2. http://ricerca.repubblica.it/repubblica/archivio/repubblica/2011/09/29/ristoranti-di-lusso-appalti-ecco-il-business.html. This is just the tip of the iceberg; at time of press the "MafiaCapitale" scandal is still unfolding. According to Marco Miccoli and Franco La Torre of the center-left Partito Democratico, "one out of five restaurants in Rome is controlled by organized crime." http://www.donellamattesini.it/index.php?option=com_content&view=article&id=1677:roma-allarme-camorra-e-ndrangheta&catid=40:blog&Itemid=111

3. Roberto Saviano, posted on 07/23/2012 at http://www.repubblica.it/cronaca/2012/07/23/news/camorra_cibi-39529644/.

4. http://www.parlafood.com

5. Anthony Majanlahti, *The Families That Made Rome.* (London: Random House. 2006)

6. Jim Tice, "The Forgotten Landscape of Rome: The Disabitato" University of Oregon, Department of Architecture, University of Oregon, ?http://nolli.uoregon.edu/disabitato.html Posted: April 15, 2005,

7. Charles Waldheim, "Notes Toward a History of Agrarian Urbanism," in Places Journal, Nov. 2010.

8. Alan Berger quoted in "Italy, a Redesign of Nature to Clean It" By

Elisabeth Rosenthal Published in New York Times: September 21, 2008

9. More than seven square meters of land per second have been consumed for more than fifty years. Growth was more intense during the 1990s when it reached ten square meters a second. http://www.cinquequotidiano.it/territori/l-inchiesta/2014/01/24/comune-di-roma-consumo-suolo-inarrestabile-dal-1956-video/

10. For another example of the privatization of public space, city authorities recently granted a noted American university exclusive access to a public park, Villa Sciarra, for a day, on the occasion of the granting of an honorable degree to Pink Floyd founder Roger Waters.

CHAPTER 3.

URBAN FABRIC: THE BUILT ENVIRONMENT

On Christmas Eve a young man with long hair and luxurious clothes inlaid with jewels kneels in prayer on a deep red stone disk laid in the floor of Saint Peter's Basilica. The Pope lifts a golden crown from the altar and places it on the man's bowed head and the throng of spectators shouts, "To Charles the August, crowned by God, great and pacific emperor, long life and victory!"

With this coronation in the year 800 the Holy Roman Empire was born, and, although the young French king did not use the title, Charlemagne is considered its first Emperor. His coronation brought some political stability to Europe and some of the first significant artistic activity in Rome since its fall. In fact, some historians, such as Kenneth Clark and Richard Krautheimer, invoking the Latin name for Charles, Carolus, have termed the period that follows the "Carolingian Renaissance."

If you left St. Peter's Basilica after the coronation, say to walk to your home on the Esquiline, you would have seen a city surprisingly similar to that of the height of the empire. Of course, the city had been devastated by numerous invasions which had stripped buildings of their valuable artworks and often left them roofless, open to the elements. Nevertheless, the basic building shapes were recognizable. Leaving St. Peter's in the direction of the Colosseum you would pass the Circus Flaminius, the Pantheon, the Theatre of Pompey and then the Baths of Agrippa. Traversing the Roman Forum through the Arch of Septimius Severus, the Forum of Trajan with its sculpted column would be visible on your right. You might detour through the Suburra neighborhood, still a working class quarter as it had been at the time of Augustus, and visit the still visible ruins of the Baths of Trajan. If you needed to shop, Trajan's markets were still active as they had been in 110 AD when they opened as the world's first planned shopping center.

Indeed, an anonymous traveller gave an account of that very route in about 800 AD. The manuscript has come down to us under the name Einsiedeln Itinerary, after the Swiss monastery where it is preserved. This is one of the first of a long tradition of such itineraries, often laid out as lists of "must sees" for the religious pilgrim seeking penitence or later for the bourgeois traveller on his or her grand tour[1]. These itineraries all describe a city whose fabric has, for the most part, been "woven," but which has fraying edges, worn spots, and a few gaping holes.

The fortified monastery of Santi Quattro Coronati, amidst the gardens of the disabitato

Good fences and the limits of growth

In *Building Thinking Dwelling*, Heideggar notes that limits are not where something ends but where something begins; "A boundary is not that at which something stops, but, as the Greeks recognized, the boundary is that from which something begins its presencing."[2]

Rome's origins are intricately tied up in this recognition of limits, ever since the legendary furrow plowed by Romulus (over which his brother Remus impertinently leaped, evoking the wrath that would end in his murder). A Roman city anywhere in the world grew through a combination of ordering lines (the *decumanus* and *cardus* and their parallel streets) and limits. The *Pomerium* was the administrative limit (marked simply with inscribed tablets, some of which can still be seen on city streets) beyond which the city ceased to exist. Joseph Rykwert writes of Roma Quadrata, that "until the end of the Republic the city would have been *quadrata* (or square) in two ways: its urban territory was divided into four districts, and its central — in constitutional, not geometric terms — areas of assembly were certainly consecrated and perhaps even geometrically regular."[3]

The notion that a boundary should carry such weight, both symbolically and functionally, is alien to us today. Sure we might take off a hat on entering a church or put on a *kippah* when entering a temple, but I tend to think of my rights as inalienable, staying with me regardless of where I go. And yet for Romans such place-based restrictions were common. A soldier ceased to be a soldier (and like everyone, had to lay down arms) upon entering the *pomerium*. Magistrates could not decree a death sentence there. A body could not be buried there.

In a similar way, time-based limits have often acted to limit absolute power, whether they be term limits, land leases, job contracts or religiously dictated periods of forgiveness. One such example in Rome is the Jubilee Year, based on the Hebrew tradition of forgiving debts every "seven times seven" years, incorporated into Christian tradition first with a fifty years repetition later shortened to twenty-five[4]. The Jubilee, like the Olympics, provides a firm temporal target which spurs productivity and innovative energy.

City Constructs or Urban Weave

Human creativity works best when pushing against physical constraints and temporal deadlines, and the built environment of Rome, what architects call "urban fabric," has emerged over the centuries within a rich and problematic set of limits indeed. In Italian "Urban Fabric" is also often translated literally as *tessuto* (or textile) to indicate a continuous weave of material that comprise a city.

The Italian noun *fabbrica* has several meanings, none of which refer precisely to textiles or cloth. When we speak of urban fabric it is not the soft malleable kind, nor is it easily portable like something you might throw in a beach bag. The verb fabricate may mean "to falsify" or "to concoct a story" but its roots lie in the manufacture of something very real and physical[5].

Fabric is what is fabricated, the result of human enterprise. Cities don't "grow" or "evolve" of their own accord, but rather are always the result of a process of fabrication, a term which does not necessarily comprise planning. And Rome, after more than 1,000 years of fabrication, has left us a big pile of physical things. If these ruined palaces, temples, basilicas and porticos were imposing, they were not indestructible.

The physical plant, and the maintenance and construction crew, of the building where Charlemagne was crowned would, in its 16th century Renaissance incarnation, all become known as the *Fabbrica di San Pietro*, a title which brings to mind smokestacks and assembly lines more than altars and cupolas.

Rossi, in his introduction to *The Architecture of the City*, speaks of "la fabbrica della città" using a word for "building" in the old Latin and Renaissance sense of man's construction as it evolves

over time[6]. For Rossi the it is essentially a collective artifact."
As a young architect, reading Rossi's Architecture of the City
was like exploring a Rome of the mind[7].

If we are serious about tackling climate change on an urbanizing
planet we need to rethink the role of urban fabric. Instead of
thinking of cities as physical artifacts– and buildings as fixed
objects– we are starting to think of them as bundles of services,
malleable and flexible. The buildings may be very solid themselves but the activities that take place within change with our
needs, desires and technological capacity. The functions inside
the Pantheon change, but its physical form persists. The fabric
of our cities provides the "hardware" for what Alex Steffen,
founder of Worldchanging, calls "augmented urbanism," the
enrichment of our cities through shared systems, software, and
additional layers of meaning.

One way of mapping this urbanism, represented by modeling
and street-view, emphasizes the three dimensional constructed
reality, the buildings and other walls that rise up from the land
and guide our movement and frame our visual field, opening vistas and blocking other realms from view. But another, the plan
view, emphasizes the city as a Roman grid or medieval web. In
less urban settings, such as North American metropolis, we tend
to map routes to follow and think of ourselves and our buildings as objects moving "on roads," while in older city centers,
designed more for people than for vehicles, we speak of being
"in roads." In America we live *on* Main Street while in England
we live *in* Market Street.

Today we are used to switching back and forth between drone's
eye satellite imagery and cars' eye street view, but any historic
map of central Rome speaks of the combined nature of the city
as fixed structure and woven fabric.

Density

In 1800 only 2.5 percent of the world's population lived in cities; the rest were in villages or rural areas. This rose to 13 percent at the start of the last century and has continued to rise ever since. We have now passed the 50 percent urban mark with predictions that by 2050 60 percent of the world's population will live in urban areas. Yet when we look closely at this urbanization, rather than being from country to city what we find is often migration from compact pedestrian-friendly mixed-use villages to the margins of sprawling metropolises. This leads us to question what we really mean by "cities," is it a question of overall population or a question of density?

In the last 50 years, as urbanized land has more than doubled, the average density of urban areas has dropped by 50 percent. Research by Peter Newman and Kenworthy shows that this low density development, which has occurred especially in US cities, is proportional to energy use; the lower the density, the higher the fuel consumption.

The critique of low-density sprawl is familiar to anyone who has read the works of Paolo Soleri, the Italian architect who left his home in Piedmont in the 1940s to work in the American Southwest and spent most of his life designing and promoting his version of compact urbanism. According to Soleri, "they literally transform the earth, turn farms into parking lots and waste enormous amounts of time and energy transporting people, goods and services over their expanses. My solution is urban implosion rather than explosion."[8]

Another Italian-born architect, Richard Rogers, has also dedicated much of his career to advocacy of compact cites. "a dense and socially diverse city where economic and social activities overlap and where communities are focused around neighborhoods." Compare the sprawl cities described by Soleri with the compact ones described by Rogers; apart from the efficiencies of the latter made possible by proximity, there are social and economic costs of sprawl. As long as the qualities of mixed-use and overlap are met, compact urbanism may refer to webs of semi-autonomous settlements with farmland between (the rural Italian model) or to a cluster of neighborhoods (the Roman model).

In Rome, density seems a given but it has radically decreased in recent decades as residents have fled the historic center. According to Stefano Boeri, one in seven homes in central Rome are uninhabited, left empty as investments. Meanwhile, rents have increased 91 percent in recent decades. The historic center of Rome was home to 370,000 people in 1951; this is now down to 100,000. Like Venice, the central district has been hollowed out and left to temporary residents or tourists, while the outlying districts, lacking in history and the complications that come with it, is booming out of control.

Mapping Eternity

No city has been mapped so obsessively and extensively as Rome, and no one knows Rome's maps as well as Allan Ceen. A cartographer, architect and life-long Romanophile, Allan has been collecting (and continues to collect and produce) maps and other prints which he safeguards and exhibits in the great room of Studium Urbis, not far from Piazza Farnese. Countless students of architecture and urban studies have had the privilege of hearing Allan expound on the evolution of graphic representation of the city from its origins to the digital present.

Any discussion of the mapping of Rome's urban fabric must begin with the Marble Plan. Etched (or rather gouged, given the huge scale and clunky medium) in the Severan period of the Roman Empire, this plan represents the entire inhabited area of Rome at a scale of 1:248. It was affixed to the wall of the Forum of Peace (the pock marks left upon its later removal are still perceptible to the left of the church of San Cosma e Damiano) visible to passersby. Documented are the public and private buildings, monuments and shops, but also the open spaces in between. Some clues suggest that the marble plan documents not just a single point in time but multiple moments, the coexistence of monuments destroyed (by fire) with contemporary structures from the Severan period. Was this due to the lag in the production of the map and difficulty in editing information carved in stone, or was there an intentionality behind representing the persistence of built form?

Maps of Rome from the fall of Rome to the dawn of the Renaissance favor the episodic and narrative over the logical or realistic. In addition to itineraries such as the Einsiedeln, there are stylized depictions of key monuments but without any buildings or public spaces in between. It is not until Leonardo Buffalini in 1551 that we will again see the city in plan view. Two centuries later GiovanBattista Nolli will make the definitive map of Rome, one that will set standards of map making for centuries. Nolli's 1748 plan systematically describes the city fabric in black and white, distinguishing the built city (black) from the spaces in between (white). Nolli makes the simple decision to represent publicly accessible spaces, whether city streets or courtyards or churches, differently from inaccessible volumes (whether structural walls and columns or entire private homes).

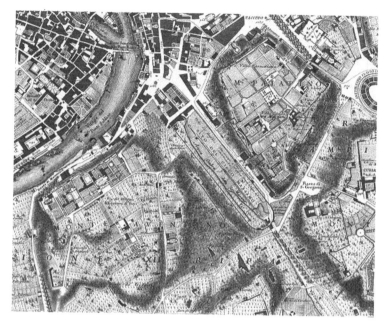

Detail of the 1748 Nolli plan

Palimpsest

Rome's historic center still today has the qualities that Nolli mapped in 1748, with the persistent palimpsests of now defunct ancient structures, such as the Stadium of Domitian, the Odeum or Pompey's Theatre. These traces are easily discernible in aerial photography, like the silhouettes of buried structures visible in photographs of desert landscapes. But rather than being buried by nature, they have been engulfed by the city, constructed over centuries but always on the same basic foundation lines. Aaron Betsky, in his article Uneternal City[9], goes so far as to say that "Rome can no longer be planned anymore than any other aspect of global sprawl can be. It can only be tracked and traced, with local interventions being about all that is possible." The many maps of Rome, he says, "represent a kind of mythic palimpsest, a place that might already be there, we have just not seen it, a Rome of our imagination that is as ephemeral as the view through the rearview mirror."

As Richard Sennett notes in "The Open City," an environment rigid in form, static in function is doomed to fail. Mankind is permanently threatened by two disasters: order and disorder and cities need a solution to both, an ordering plan and an insurgency against excessive order.

Cities provide for this kind of complexity naturally, through radical adjacencies and proximity. Now what Soleri called the "urban effect" can be fabricated digitally, counterfeited in a place where no city exists. Thus technology does not always have an urbanizing effect; in fact often it isolates in the name of connecting. Even in cities we have become a culture of individuals plugged into devices, tuned into a distant network but ignoring the reality around us. Like the tourist with her face in the guidebook oblivious to the work of art in front of her, we experience reality through a screen. We neglect to "live in the present," one of Douglas Rushkoff's commands for the digital age. Technology, or more precisely Web 2.0 part and parcel with various platforms of social networking, now allows us to carry out much of what previously required proximity: socializing, information-gathering, debate, commerce, entertainment, recreation.

Twelve centuries after Charlemagne, you can still duck into a little church built in his reign: Santa Prassede on the Esquiline Hill. A few blocks from Termini Station in a neighborhood now a melting pot of Asians, Africans and other recent immigrants, you are transmitted back into the 9th century. In the dimly lit basilica you gaze up at the apse mosaics glittering with gold and other rich colors. There, alongside St. Peter, Paul, and the patron saint of this church, Prassede, you will see Pasquale I, the Pope who commissioned this building so many centuries ago, carrying the model of his church. The city that Charlemagne arrived at in '800 was already ancient, but it was at the same time brand new. Pop a euro in the box to turn on the lights in the chapel the Pope built for his mother, Saint Teodora, and, if you want to learn more, the airwaves passing through the ancient walls carry more information to your smartphone than contained in all the libraries of the 9th century world.

The torn *tessuto* of Rome invites continued fabrication, but most of the opportunities today demand not starting from scratch but fixing and fitting, not planning but mapping, not remaking the physical but rethinking the flows of data and energy that pass unstoppable through the walls of our cities.

Via Giulia and San Giovanni dei Fiorentini

Notes

1. Other important such documents include the *Mirabilia*, originally composed by Benedetto Canonico, cantor of the basilica of S. Pietro, between 1140 and 1143.

2. Martin Heideggar, *Building, Dwelling, Thinking* (New York: Harper Colophon Books, 1971)

3. Joseph Rykwert, The Idea of a Town: The Anthropology of Urban Form in Rome, Italy and the Ancient World (London: Faber and Faber, 2011), 62.

4. Occasionally, as Francis did for 2016, a Pope will declare a special Jubilee in between the planned ones.

5. In Italian the word "fabbrica" most commonly refers to factory (a word whose ostensible translation as "fattoria" causes no small confusion, as this actually means "farm").

6. Aldo Rossi, *Architecture of the City*. Cambridge, MA: MIT Press, 1982. 18

7. I had the privilege to meet and talk with Rossi at a Harvard GSD event in around 1990. Our conversation is a bit of a haze—clouded by many glasses of red wine and my own nervousness at speaking (in Italian, no less) with the most influential architect of that generation. We spoke of Rome and of the permanence of buildings and I thanked him for helping me to understand the richness of history, separating buildings from their functional roles to see them as part of cycles of change.

8. Paolo Soleri, interview in "The Evolution of the City" in *The Urban Ideal*, (Albany, CA: Berkeley Hill Books, 2004)

9. Betsky, Aaron, ed. *Uneternal City: Urbanism Beyond Rome.* Catalogue of exhibit of 2008 Biennale di Architettura.

CHAPTER 4.

ENERGY: THE POWER OF ROME

The sun in Rome in the Summer is an intense, direct, persistent and memorable source of light and heat. It is Mediterranean, almost African. Buildings become defined with sharp lines and deep shadows. The hot sun lends added significance to pine trees and colonnades and brings huge respect for catacombs, crypto-porticos, stone churches and any structure built into the earth, the contrasting coolness of which becomes an asset. As you pass from the glaring midday sun of the Piazza della Rotonda to stand, dwarfed, amidst the massive granite monoliths which support the roof of the Pantheon, the temperature drops dramatically, the tile roof filters out the rays, and the 20-foot thick concrete walls and well-preserved ancient marble floor absorb the heat from your body. Enter the building now through the bronze doors and your eye returns to the sunlight entering through a precise circular "oculus" at the top of the perfectly hemispherical concrete dome. The contrast between the hot and chaotic city and the cool geometric interior surprises you as it has visitors for over 2,000 years. Whereas out in the piazza the sunlight encompassed you, now it is precisely focused in a spotlight on the floor, a circle of light which moves slowly but perceptibly from hour to hour and season to season. Return later in the day and it will slide across the trapezoidal coffer pattern of the dome until sunset, when it flickers and is gone.

Rome's ancient buildings embody an awareness of the sun's apparent movement across the skies. The sunlight penetrating the oculus of the Pantheon marks the passage of hours and seasons, passing from the upper hemisphere through the semicircular arch above the portal to descend again into the lower hemisphere at precisely midday on the spring equinox. On this date at the end of the winter season, the sun penetrates the grille above the door and begins to illuminate the floor of the portico from the inside. A month later, on April 21st (Rome's traditional founding day) the full disk illuminates the floor outside the door. The ancient Roman historian Cassius Dio tells us that the Pantheon was dedicated to all the gods "because of its vaulted roof, it actually resembles the heavens.[1]"

A few hundred yards away, the point of the 60 foot tall obelisk called the *orologeum* (from the Latin word for hour) casts its shadow in a precise rhythm on the modern pavement outside Italy's Houses of Parliament. I recently climbed with a small group of travelers down to see the one small section visible of the original surface onto which it projected its shadow. The white stone contains mathematical markings in Greek and symbols of the signs of the zodiac, a veritable solar calendar.

Rome's urban layout, its building designs and their details, can teach us and inspire us as we again begin to recognize the importance of adapting our built environment to climate (after several decades of eluding ourselves that our technology made such adaptation unnecessary). Another example: the great cloth canopy topping the Colosseum, called "velarium" after the *vela* or sails on which the technology was based, provided comfort for its occupants in the summer months. According to Seutonius, the emperor Caligula saw in the hot summer sun an opportunity to inflict pain and "would sometimes draw back the awnings when the sun was hottest and give orders that no one be allowed to leave," a captivating illustration of the power of the sun, and the cruelty of this emperor.

These same buildings were supposed to inspire us because they embody meaning and cultural knowledge. We are beginning to see that they can inspire us for another reason: their common sense approaches to climate. From the radiant-heating ducts below Ostia Antica to the cutting-edge photovoltaic installations on the rooftops of central Rome, most of the energy a thriving modern city needs is already there for the taking.

Firmitas and Thermal Delight

Reyner Banham was one of the first authors to focus on this other, less photogenic aspect of building in his 1969 book, *The Architecture of the Well-tempered Environment*, which provides an encyclopedic introduction to the topic of thermal systems. The following year Lisa Hershong's *Thermal Delights in Archi-*

tecture addressed the more sensual aspects of the same. But two millennia earlier the architect Vitruvius was already preaching the importance of thermal performance in design choices. "The method of building which is suited to Egypt would be very improper in Spain, and that in use in Pontus would be absurd at Rome: so in other parts of the world a style suitable to one climate, would be very unsuitable to another: for one part of the world is under the sun's course, another is distant from it, and another, between the two, is temperate.[2]" Roman homes, whether the single-family *domus* that we find in sites like Pompeii or the multi-story *insula,* tenement houses prominent in working class neighborhoods of Ostia Antica, were built with thermal qualities in mind.

At 42 degrees latitude and close to the Mediterranean, which acts as a heat sink, Rome has a temperate climate. It is hot and dry in the summer and chilly and damp in the winter, free from the extremes of cold of northern Europe and the parching droughts of the equator. Even in winter, the sun at midday often provides enough radiant heat to warm a massive masonry wall which, in turn, radiates this warmth to its inhabitants into the night. Similarly, in the summer, the walls discharge the midday heat at night and in the morning are ready to start absorbing energy again, resulting in remarkably cool interiors (as we experienced in the Pantheon). For millennia Rome was designed around a precise awareness of the changing presence of the sun throughout the day and the seasons.

Roman baths such as the Forum Baths of Ostia had hot rooms, called *caldaria,* opening to the south to receive low winter sunlight which would be absorbed by dark colored stone walls and floors, while the cooler *frigidaria* baths ensured shading from the high summer sun and breezes which would produce an evaporative cooling effect when passing over the pools of cool water. Siting and smart design alone was not enough to provide thermal comfort. In the winter it was supplemented by wood burning fires, whose scalding water would fill the tubs and hot fumes would pass through hollow walls to radiate warmth directly to bathers before venting out into the air.

Drawing a Bath

It is another "hotter than normal" September day and a group of sweaty and suntanned students from one of Boston's prominent university architecture programs are sprawled out on the ground in an elite bathing club. There is no water, and the hot Mediterranean sun is beating down on them relentlessly, but the students are thrilled nevertheless. They are spending a week at ancient Rome's port city of Ostia Antica, producing precise measured drawings of the ruined Baths of Mitra. One of a half-a-dozen bath complexes in the teeming seaside town, these baths were part of the social amenities surrounding the Mythrean religion, a mysterious cult that emerged at the height of the Empire and was eclipsed as Christianity moved to the forefront in the 4th century. The drawings will enrich the collective archives of archaeological data about this still-emerging site and the students' work, in addition to providing them with an unforgettable learning experience, will award them academic credits toward their professional degree in architecture.

The word "thermal" corresponds to the Roman word for bath: *terme*. Rome's original Termini station was built above the remains of the Baths of Diocletian, thus its name (not, as many assume, because the trains terminate there). On chilly winter days thermal baths were the only places that were heated, and an hour or so relaxing in the warmth of the *caldarium* (or, at Hadrian's Villa, in the *Heliocaminus* or solar sauna) would make the rest of one's day more bearable. In the baths of Mitras at Ostia, as in the Forum Baths nearby, remains of each of these are visible. The heated spaces are easily recognizable by the crawl spaces under the floor and hollow tile walls through which smoke and hot air from the fires below passed, radiating heat to the bathers within. Seeking respite from the hot sun, our students explored the cisterns and surface ducts below ground, where the temperatures stay constantly cool. This simple "geothermal" fact — below ground temperatures remain nearly constant — informed many baths and palaces of the ancient world. It has been nearly forgotten today.

Measuring and drawing at Ostia Antica

Performative Antiquities

Earlier in the semester we analyzed the energy performance of the Domus of the Fortuna Annonaria based on hypothetical reconstructions of its roofs and porticos, demonstrating it to be a successful exemplar of passive solar heating and natural ventilation. The workshop then proposed a contemporary transformation of the ancient house into a museum, augmenting the ancient energy strategies with today's best practice and technologies to achieve a carbon zero ecological footprint. The results are beautiful, and confirm our hypothesis that the bulk of energy performance depends, not on the latest German or Japanese high-tech gizmos, but on basic, common sense design. A south-facing portico shades the hot summer sun but welcomes the desirable low winter rays. Thick masonry walls provide thermal mass to mitigate day-night temperature swings, capturing the sun's energy during the day to radiate it at night when the temperature drops. Gushing fountains trigger the evaporative cooling effect, absorbing heat in the process of converting water to vapor.

Calling this traditional Roman house carbon neutral would be going too far. The ruins the students are documenting may seem comprised of only durable, recyclable materials such as concrete, brick and stone, but look closer and you see the square holes where wood scaffolding, floor beams and roof rafters once sat. Large quantities of wood were also squandered to built the ships that brought the slabs of polished marble facing from quarries as far afield as North Africa and Asia Minor. Wood was burned in the production of the bricks which formed an integral part of the concrete structural system, now revealed where facing stone and stucco has been lost. During the course of the Roman Empire the forests of Tuscany were not-so-gradually transformed into the naked rolling hills travelers love today. This "imbedded energy" load that the students calculated was offset to some degree by longevity: instead of the 20-year life span of 20th century buildings, the materials in this Roman house were re-used again and again, a practice that has, thankfully, once again become the norm today.

The Beauty of Contrasts

One of the lessons of Rome lies in the beauty of contrasts, including thermal contrasts. The ancient builder's command of means to achieve thermal comfort didn't mean that anyone, even the most affluent, expected a constant, standard temperature. Far from it. The ritual of the Roman bath is a case in point: a plunge in cold water followed by a rub down, a hot sponge bath, a steam bath and, again, cold water. Certainly in the winter, when central Italy is chilly and humid, an hour or so spent in a hot, dry sauna, combined with vigorous exercise and warm layers of wool made for an acceptable, if not entirely comfortable, routine, especially when activities were concentrated in the warmer midday and afternoon hours. By contrast, in the summer only a fool would be anywhere but resting in the shade in the hot midday hours; productive activities took place (and to a lesser degree still do today) in the early morning hours and well into the evening when the city cools down noticeably.

For years I've watched public spaces in Rome– and people's use of them– change as the seasons change. In the winter the sunny side is where people gather, where sidewalk cafes prosper, street furniture materializes on warm days and people emerge from cool stone *palazzi* into the warmth of sun-drenched public space. The opposite occurs during the summer. It is now the shade and shadows which draw all but the most thoughtless tourists; where shade is not already provided by buildings or trees, umbrellas appear or shutters are drawn during daylight hours (only to be reopened, when the sun goes down, to maximize cool evening breezes and vent out any heat absorbed during the day).

Watching the dress patterns is indicative as well. As soon as temperatures drop slightly, even as tourists are still in t-shirts, fur coats and down parkas appear. But even on the hottest summer day it is rare to see a Roman man in shorts. It may be that Italians have a higher tolerance for heat than for the lack of it, or a lower tolerance for male anatomy than for female (skimpy dresses yes, men's shorts no). The spaces one occupies in most American cities are either indoors, fully-conditioned year-round, or outdoors whereas in European cities there are more intermediate spaces, inside but not sealed from the elements. These spaces, whether the stairwells or entrance halls of apartment buildings or the galleria shopping arcades, act as buffers between the interior and the elements.

In Boston I was used to spending time in overheated interiors and putting on a heavy coat only for the short jaunts between destinations, or not at all when a short walk across campus in a t-shirt was a refreshing contrast. In Rome where big stone interiors tend to stay chilly the attitude is to heat the body, not the building. Radiant heat works along these principles, whether provided by in-floor heating coils, wood-burning fireplaces or simply well-placed windows. The explanation for the summer dress code is more complicated; instead of cooling the body in the face of heat (for which the solutions are more invasive) Romans avoid the heat by shifting their daily routines. Thus they tend to dress for the cooler hours, especially the evenings, while the tourist dresses for the hottest hours and suffers anyway, only to feel out of place and often downright chilly once the sun goes down.

Another example of cultural approaches to energy that I have always found enlightening is the drying of clothes. Since moving to Rome I have never had a dryer, though our washing machines have always been the most sophisticated high-performance devices which leave clothes immaculately clean with a minimum of water and energy. And then we hang the clothes to dry on a line or a rack. One of the most common observations I've heard from North American travellers has always been about this lack of dryers, with clothes-lines often associated with poverty of the trailer park variety. The clothes drying paradox: in the US we burn petroleum or coal ("ancient sunlight" as Thomas Hartmann calls it) to produce electrical current, then transmit that electricity (wastefully) over long distances, and finally transform it back into heat and power to turn a drum to dry our clothes. Or we can simply hang them out to dry in the sun and air. Italians prefer the latter, (although a good advertising campaign might convince them to change their ways as it has convinced them to parrot other wasteful American foibles, buying ever larger cars and homes).

Personally I find the ritual of hanging laundry, like that of tending a garden or taking a walk, a great way of ensuring contact with the outside air. I agree, however, with those who balk at hanging clean clothes over polluted city streets. Like the argument against urban gardens, this is all the more reason to address the core problems. The solution is not to limit our exposure to air pollution; it is to eliminate the causes of pollution (especially Rome's automobile addiction, as we will discuss later).

Let There Be Light

"Show me the apartment that lets you sleep! In this city sleep costs millions, and that's the root of the trouble. The wagons thundering past through those narrow twisting streets, the oaths of draymen caught in a traffic-jam, would rouse a dozing seal—or an emperor." So Juvenal describes Rome of the late first and early second centuries AD. One had to choose to either shut out the noise by closing wooden shutters and risking suffocation, or leave them open and stay awake all night.

Until relatively recently, the choice to let in light most often meant a sacrifice in thermal insulation, which had to be compensated for by high fuel consumption. The single-glazed curtain walls of the post-war office buildings are as distant from the high-performance glazing we have today as they were from ancient Roman shuttered window walls. While good solar designers have been exploring the potential of the "positive greenhouse effect" for decades, taking advantage of the unique properties of glass, like certain gases in our planet's atmosphere, to allow light to penetrate but prevent heat transfer. As our technological evolution would have it, our ability to profit from this effect only came at the moment when our exploitation of (seemingly) cheap fossil fuels made it (seemingly) un-necessary. Recently this situation has changed and the technology of glazing, now no less energy efficient than masonry, has received the attention and the application it deserves.

It has been confusing to laypeople and to many architects themselves to see the use of glass walls shift, in one generation, from environmental heresy to high-performance energy savers. In cities from Bilbao to Berlin it is common to see new glass walls clipped in front of old masonry ones, second skins which mediate between outside and in, or simply double glass envelopes which let in light and heat when desired but reflect or vent it away when unwanted. This "garment architecture" approach, to use Paolo Soleri's term, would make as much sense in Rome's variable climate and a few examples can be found. The retrofitting of the Lazio Region's offices by Aldo Aymonino, the Dutch Embassy, or a recent (unpublished) proposal by A+V Architetti to offset the power load of Rome's MAXXI Museum by applying a photovoltaic greenhouse to one of the adjacent masonry buildings are just a few examples. Renzo Piano's glazed porticos surrounding the Parco della

Musica incorporate operable textile shades, intended to allow light and warmth in the winter while keeping the hot summer sun from hitting the building's walls. Even Massimiliano Fuksas's muscular megastructure called *La Nuvola* (the "cloud") attempts to mitigate the impact of suspending Rome's new convention center inside a big glass box by giving the box a double skin. One inspiring example of a performative facade in Rome remains Luigi Moretti's Casa Girasole (sunflower house), dating to the late 1940s. Its windows peel off the screen-like facade like flower petals to catch light and views while sliding shutters, operated by the building's users, result in a constantly changing appearance. Like sunflowers turning to face their energy source, or crawling ivy providing Rome's *palazzi* a variable second skin, biomimicry has been providing obvious solutions as long as humans have been building.

Natural lighting has long been supplemented, if not displaced, by artificial lighting. Limited use of artificial lighting didn't have to wait until the gas lamps of the streets of Victorian cities, later replaced by electricity. One of the most common finds in Roman archaeological digs is the small oil-burning lamp, often affixed to walls of darker corridors or carried by hand through the rooms after hours. Not only a functional necessity — it was far more practical to simply carry on activities during the day and sleep at night —sometimes artificial lighting was used to literally highlight artifacts, to see the city under a different light.[3]

Casa Girasole, architect Luigi Moretti 1949

Green is the New Gold

When asked about what makes architecture "sustainable" most people will mention energy conservation and renewable sources of power before bringing up the other six themes of sustainable urbanism. Between buildings and transportation cities consume close to 80 percent of all energy. Most of central Rome, though, was built prior to the harnessing of fossil fuels for heating, cooling, lighting and transport; it worked pretty well and there is a lot we can learn from it. In his presentation of the 2030 challenge architect Edward Mazria notes that, before resorting to the purchase of energy from (costly) renewable sources or the application of (costly) technological solutions such as photovoltaics, wind generators, automated sun shading devices and the like, buildings can already cut their energy consumption dramatically by doing what we designers do, that is designing responsively to local conditions.

Thanks to its temperate climate and mostly well-planned historical building stock, Rome has what it takes to become a demonstration project for the net zero energy city without a huge investment, through smart retrofits and design.

Sometime in the late 2000s renewable energy passed from the terrain of the radical green counter culture to corporate mainstream, a fact I first realized at the Zero Emissions Rome trade fair a few years ago.

Two huge pavilions were dedicated to "sun" and "sun/earth" —the latter seemed to result from the fact that there were so many exhibitors in the solar energy field that one pavilion was not enough, but they shared space with green chemical companies and the like. Another was dedicated to wind, and a fourth that I didn't make it to was supposed to address carbon neutrality.

I spent most of my morning looking at photovoltaic panels, by far the biggest sector of the growing market. Italy ranks fifth as producer of electricity through photovoltaic cells, after Germany, Japan, Spain and the United States. To date almost 400 megawatts of production capacity has been installed here; in Europe as a whole the number is about 90 gigawatts (thanks mostly to Germany). This may still sound small compared to the multi terawatt capacity of nuclear and hydroelectric plants in Europe, but it is growing rapidly. Italy has been slow to jump on the bandwagon but thanks to a combination of high government incentives, the most costly electricity in Europe, and its sunny climate, the boot is finally showing some interest in photovoltaics. Strangely, the region where it is most productive is Lombardia, not among the sunniest, but sunny and southern Puglia is in second place. The reason has to do with confused regulations, differing from region to region, in place of a much needed national guideline.

Lacking was any serious attention to the design of photovoltaic panels: just the standard rigid panel composed of 50-100 cells. It seems like the days that computers were big grey boxes and monitors flickered with green text. Design was evident in the marketing materials (some great graphics and nice stand design) but not in the products or their representatives who from their looks could have just as easily been selling tractors or pharmaceuticals. While some stands showed sophisticated fastening systems and transparent glass panels without the ubiquitous aluminum frame, there was no real cutting edge application of the technology on display. And worse, none of it was put to use despite the sunny day. As far as I could tell there were megawatts worth of panels on display but the entire fair was being powered by the national grid. Did anyone even think of putting all these panels to use to demonstrate their functionality? I suppose that would be like suggesting that an automotive show actually had cars with their engines on; a logistic nightmare not to mention health hazard as well.

On a similar note, the *Fiera di Roma* (the convention center where the show was held) is — from an urban standpoint — one of the worst buildings that could have been built in the current age of environmental crisis. Located far on the edge of town, near the airport, it was made for cars and in fact is surrounded by a sea of parking like any suburban shopping mall. Instead of being built adjacent to the Rome-airport train line it was placed just far enough away to require a shuttle bus to make the rounds, a degrading, polluting and time-consuming experience.

Interior of Pantheon dome

Net-Zero Cities

By 2030 3/4 of the world's energy will be consumed in urbanized areas; it is in cities that the greatest opportunity exists to wean us off our dependence on fossil fuels like oil which we consume thousands of times faster than its rate of production. The alternatives exist, most evidently the sun. One hour of sunlight at high noon contains the energy used by the entire planet in a year. To benefit from this wealth of energy, buildings must be rethought, no longer considered consumers of energy but potential power plants.

Rome is well-situated to become one of Europe's first net-zero energy cities. In Rome's temperate climate, leveraging emerging photovoltaic technologies and good, common-sense design, the area occupied by an urban building can provide for all that building's energy needs and even produce a surplus to feed into the power grid. The energy efficiency of the city's building stock must be recognized, appreciated and augmented where possible, an investment that has no downside.

In cold weather Rome has a great opportunity to exploit adjacencies for co-generation. My condominium complex went through several cold winters when the central heating wasn't activated due to bickering about policy, but meanwhile the industrial bakery on the ground floor continued to vent hot air to the atmosphere, air which channeled intelligently could have heated most of the building. For true cold-weather performance a good deal of retrofitting is needed, especially the application of thermal insulation, air-tight glazing and weather seals but this can be done gradually as new products and techniques become available. It doesn't have to be a big investment and it doesn't necessarily require sophisticated technology.

In the past, keeping your building comfortable often allowed (or required) active participation on the part of the users. Is this really a bad thing? Pulling the shutters closed as the afternoon sun strikes a facade and opening them as the evening breezes kick in, these are some of Roman life's greatest rituals, on a par with the late morning espresso. Would we really prefer the monotony of regulated air conditioning, even if it had no environmental impact?

Every aspect of sustainable city living carries an energy cost. It takes energy to transport and process water, and even when electricity is produced through hydroelectric generators the net gain is often outweighed, as with nuclear power, by losses in transmission from distant sources. About half of the energy consumed in cities is due to our buildings, the urban fabric addressed in Chapter 3. Vegetation as discussed in Chapter 2 not only provides an efficient natural buffer to reduce building's energy load and the surrounding heat-island effect; local agriculture preserves huge quantities of fossil fuels that would be spent on transport and fertilizers. Over 30 percent of the energy used in cities is due to our transportation choices which will be addressed in Chapter 6. I have discussed here how shared public spaces act as thermally attractive buffers, boosting both energy savings and community ties. But it is the connection to waste that is perhaps the most direct; we discard materials that contain embodied energy and, rather than exploiting their energy content, we often bury them, leaving a hazard for future generations. This is the subject of the next chapter: waste.

Notes

1. Cassius Dio, 53.27.2

2. Vitruvius, The Ten Books of Architecture, translated by Morris Hickey Morgan (New York: Dover, 1960)

3. Goethe described a torchlight visit to the Vatican or Capitoline museums as a visit desired alike by all strangers, artists and connoisseurs.

CHAPTER 5.

WASTE: ROME'S ECONOMY OF REUSE

I am inside a cylindrical structure, about two meters deep and a bit less in diameter. Squatting at the bottom to examine the lower surface I glance up to see the towering structures of the imperial palaces on the Palatine Hill, framed in the circular opening above.

My assignment is to make a drawing of the surfaces of the walls, rough bricks partially coated with what appears to be vitrified stone. The non-profit institute I helped launch — and headed for several years — has partnered with Stanford and Oxford universities to carry out field research at the base of the Palatine Hill, behind the Temple of Castor and Pollux and along the *Vicus Tuscus*, an ancient road of Etruscan origins connecting the Tiber river to the Roman Forum. As architect for the project I move from trench to trench, drawing plans and sections while young archaeologists work in the dust with trowels and brushes, collecting their finds in ziplock bags.

My training has prepared me to represent on paper my proposals for the future, and to document existing conditions in preparation for renovations, but documenting the past *as it is revealed* is a new experience. Instead of a single phase there are many, and the lines between them are hard to discern. It is challenging to "reconstruct" the building sequence while deconstructing the stratigraphy, and to do so without destroying the very object of study. The students from California, in particular, work slowly, in awe of the age of the fragments they uncover, and fearful of making irreversible mistakes on a site which has seen two millennia of human occupation.

Their concerns are not unfounded. At one point on about the third day of the dig the archaeologist from Oxford gives an "impromptu" speech he has probably made on countless digs. Holding a ziplock bag he removes a small pottery fragment and announces that it has been erroneously archived in the wrong context, a mistake which could have contaminated all the data and resulted in a serious misreading. With a dramatic gesture he lobs the offending terra-cotta artifact, now a meaningless scrap, onto the trash heap while the offending student (mercifully un-named) and colleagues absorb the seriousness of the crime. What I take away from the lesson is this: what counts is not the material, but the information it represents.

In the well-like structure I am drawing in the archaeological dig, the surfaces are rough and dirty, clearly not designed for human habitation. The material melted onto the walls was the result of extreme temperatures reducing marble to its component parts, removing the carbon and oxygen from calcium carbonate to produce a material commonly known as quick lime. I am at the bottom of a medieval lime kiln, many of which were constructed in the heart of Rome to reduce ancient masterpieces to cheap construction material.

Alongside the kiln are chunks of carved marble, column capitals, fragments of sculpture. Regular blocks could be reused directly in construction but decoration reduced the value, leaving them useless except to burn for lime. Today we cringe to think of such waste, but I suspect our grandchildren will react the same way when told that we squandered millions of years of carbon reserves to drive our cars to the mall.

The finds that the young English and American archaeologists brush lovingly are pieces so bereft of value that they weren't worth the effort to remove, or perhaps they ended up here when the Forum was a waste heap and cow pasture. Much fine marble would be reused either in situ, for example in the conversion of an ancient temple into a church as happened to the Pantheon in the year 609, or more commonly elsewhere, carried to a nearby job site to hold up a medieval basilica. While the *calcarari* reduced marble to its chemical components, the *marmorari* salvaged, cut, polished and reassembled the stone to produce new floors and decoration, especially in churches. In the 6th century, as vestiges of the formerly grand civilization that was Rome lay crumbling on the seven hills, whatever didn't find a feasible second life would just stand there until nature took its course. In 1845 Faustino Corsi made a list of all the marble columns known in Rome to have survived from antiquity; there were 7,012 in total![1]

Medieval Rome in particular was marked by an innovative use of pre-owned materials, transformed through skilled labor into new forms. The Cosmati family of Trastevere, for example, took broken fragments of marble and other fine stones, splitting and slicing them into usable tiles to assemble in new patterns. You can see their handiwork today, almost as good as "new," in churches like Santa Maria in Cosmedin or Santa Maria in Trastevere.

Medieval lime kiln in the Roman Forum

Harvesting Pollution

Buckminster Fuller once said that "pollution is nothing but resources we're not harvesting." In nature there is no waste and no pollution, only nutrient cycles. If we think of things as "waste" we throw them out, if we recognize value in them we find a way to reuse them. One of the most vivid examples is the culinary tradition of the *quinto quarto*, or "fifth quarter," where Roman delicacies are born of the creative use of every edible part of the animal processed in the slaughterhouses of Testaccio. Especially in times of hardship, such as the dark ages or Apollo missions gone awry, humans prove themselves highly creative in discovering new uses for discarded materials. Limits make us smarter.

Walk around Rome and you discover everywhere ingenious examples of re-use. On a recent visit to an excavation north of the city we examined the remains of a fullonica, an ancient laundry, which used urine with its ammoniac solution as a bleaching agent. Some evidence suggests that, rather than presenting waste management problems, public latrines were profitable businesses — their "product" could be sold to farmers as fertilizer and laundries as bleach. And, of course, organic waste found a second life, feed for domestic animals or simply compost.

Construction waste, which makes up 25 percent of our rubbish today, did not exist in ancient Rome. Marble, imported at a huge expense from distant quarries, was used in its entirety. Irregular scraps left over after the cutting of large regular blocks and slabs could always be shaped into small mosaic *tesserae* and assembled into functional and decorative floors which can still be seen all over sites like Ostia Antica. The left over scrapings could then be reduced to marble dust, mixed with cement and used as filler in inlaid marble decorations. Random stones and discarded brick fragments could always find a new home in the concrete conglomerate which comprises most imperial buildings; it's not uncommon to find a hand or foot imbedded in an ancient concrete wall, not the result of criminal vendetta, but the smart reuse of broken statuary.

Stratigraphy

Demolished buildings, reduced to masonry rubble and — unlike our modern construction — devoid of toxic materials, could be safely used as landfill to raise the city foundations to higher, more salubrious heights above the flooding Tiber. Grant Heiken estimates that 93 million cubic meters of man-made debris has accumulated within the Aurelian Walls over the centuries, leaving the ancient city foundations at least two to five meters, sometimes as much as 15 meters, below modern world. You might assume that this happened after the fall of Rome, and it is true that from the 5th century onward large tracts of the city were abandoned and transformed by collapsed buildings, silt from the Tiber, and rampant vegetation. But the ground was already rising during the Roman Empire. Peer down into the excavations undertaken by Mussolini at Largo Argentina and observe grey tuff stone steps buried beneath white travertine paving and carved bases of temples that disappear into the ground below other ancient stones[2]. As you stare into the sunken site at the ruins, cats and detritus of centuries of urban transformation, any simplistic notions of "original" make way for a more holistic understanding of layers and cycles. What we so nonchalantly call "ancient" was about 1500 years of evolution, during which the city changed shape and most importantly changed its ground elevation repeatedly. Like a parchment, erased and rewritten again and again, Rome represents a rich palimpsest.

Recycling in the Ghetto

Not far from Largo Argentina, in Rome's former Jewish ghetto (still Jewish, though by no means a "ghetto" in the sense of an area to which a minority group is relegated) everywhere you see testament to the restrictions enforced by the papacy from the 16th until the late 19th centuries. Following centuries of persecutions, restrictions on property, ban on professions, obligatory participation in humiliating public spectacles and the like, a Papal Bull of 1442 forbade Jews from practicing professions and working any new materials. As a result, the community became known for innovative uses for old material, especially metals and cloth. Metal scavenged from the structural supports of buildings such as the Colosseum or "discarded" by wealthier classes was molded and hammered into new shapes. Just as paper would be reused for writing and canvases painted onto again and again, cloth could be reworked almost infinitely. Old clothes were cut into small segments, like the stone tiles of the Cosmati, and restitched into beautiful decorative torah covers (*Bein Gavra*), many of which are on display in the museum of Rome's main synagogue. Today jewelry shops and fabric stores abound in the neighborhood between the Tiber Island and Largo Argentina, descendants of these ventures born of limits.

The Eighth Hill of Rome

While dining on *offal* at Flavio al Velavevodetto, not far from the slaughterhouse in Testaccio, you may notice the glass cases containing an array of broken pottery. In fact, you are looking into the ancient mound of discarded amphora, known as Monte dei Cocci or Monte Testaccio. Rome's first landfill anticipates modern waste management strategies of piling it up and burying it. But the hundred-foot high hill is composed solely of broken amphora, not the "monstrous hybrids" of our modern dumps, to use the term coined by Michael Braungart and William McDonough in *Cradle to Cradle*. Over time it has found smart re-use. The mound is conveniently porous enough to allow carving out workshops and storerooms.

In other sites, amphora never even made it to the landfill, being re-used to lighten the load of concrete domes over the Mausoleum of Helena and other structures. But the vessels designed to carry olive oil contained biological buildup which would contaminate construction sites; instead it was sprinkled with lime to render it inert and laid systematically in layers to form the mound we see today. What was once waste is now valuable real estate in the center of the city.

As an added benefit, the porous mass provides for natural heating and cooling, making it a traditional location for wine cellars and a destination for summer evening festivals, chilled by the air filtering through the terra-cotta mound. Monte Testaccio is under investigation by a team of Spanish archaeologists whose findings shed light on the swings in productivity over time in the same way tree rings provide evidence of climatic swings. The ancient landfill is a valuable testament to the economy of the Roman Empire.

By contrast, everyday thousands of tons of what just yesterday was we called "goods" and paid good money to "consume" are piled onto trucks and taken to "waste treatment facilities." For the past decades, waste management in Rome has meant one place and one man: Malagrotta, the property of Manlio Cerroni. Until its closure in 2013, 5,000 tons of trash would show up every day at what was Europe's largest landfill. Some of it would be converted to energy through incineration or gasification, but the rest just piled up. And since 2008 this landfill has been, well, full. The proposed alternatives, a new dump site north of Rome at Allumiere, or Grottaferrata in the Alban Hills, or even within the limits archaeological area of Hadrian's Villa, have all been rejected, leaving the question open.

The real problem isn't finding another landfill site but reducing, and eventually eliminating, the waste produced. The Lazio region as a whole produces over 3 million tons of waste a year, with an average of only 30 percent recycled. Compare this to Germany's 70 percent rate. The process is marred at every step: inadequate measures for separating waste in the home, at the curb, ineffective control at the processing plant leading to potentially usable recycled materials being sent to landfill anyway. The lessons of Naples, where trash piled uncollected on the streets tarnished decades of hard-earned improvements in the city's public image, seem to go unheeded in the Italian capital. The *terre del fuoco* phenomena of the Neapolitan countryside, where residents and criminal organizations have taken to burning waste (with resulting toxic emissions), has become a reality in Rome. From the cupola of Saint Peter's, where white smoke announces the election of new popes during conclave, one can see plumes of toxic black smoke rising from the countryside, a gripping symbol that a lasting solution has yet to be been found for Rome's practical waste management crisis.

Adaptive Reuse in Rome's Teatro di Marcello

Adaptive Reuse

It is fitting that Testaccio is at the hub of a neighborhood which has seen some of the major adaptive reuse projects in Rome of the past decades. From the edge of the planned social housing of Garbatella, along the Via Ostiense and across the Tiber to the former soap factories in the Marconi quarter and the old papal arsenal near Porta Portese, the southern side of Rome is replete with abandoned industrial sites either undergoing or awaiting transformation.

The phenomena of gentrification we know from New York's meat-packing district or London's Canary Wharf is nothing new. Already in the late 1st century BCE Julius Caesar, realizing that the city was growing and its former edge was no longer central, began constructing a theatre where river docks had stood, moving the industrial ports further out of town to the west. Completed a generation later by his successor Augustus, who named it after his nephew, the Theater of Marcellus is at the heart of a new cultural center planned where warehouses and markets had stood decades earlier.

The theatre still stands between the Capitoline Hill and the Tiber, although its stage, which stood near where the embankments would later be built, collapsed long ago. Its architecture was copied from the Greek building type with a few Roman modifications, the most significant being its imposing freestanding position above the Tiber flood plains rather than being nested into the landscape, as Greek theaters always were. The structure is of concrete, dressed in the Greek architectural orders: Doric at the base, then Ionic, then Corinthian, exactly as used on the Colosseum a century later. Inside, the three tiers of bleachers could accommodate up to 20,000 spectators for performances of (mostly Greek) theatrical productions, both comedies and tragedies.

The Theatre of Marcellus was never demolished but rather lived on as the city's quintessential example of adaptive reuse. Like the Colosseum and many other massive Roman structures after the city's decline and fall, the theater's arcades provided shelter for vagrants who moved closer to the river after the destruction of the aqueducts made it impossible to live on the hills far from any source of water. Powerful families took possession of these sites and fought to maintain control during the middle ages. The Frangipane family lorded over the ruins of the Colosseum, the Colonna fought their rivals in the Campus Martius, and the Theatre of Marcellus fell under the control alternately of the Caetani and Savelli and Orsini families. In 1550 the Savelli commissioned Sienese Architect Baldassare Peruzzi to create for them a respectable palace on the site and, in a surprisingly modern approach to cultural heritage, rather than demolish the theater, he used it as the foundations. I have had the good fortune to visit much of the building on various occasions, when the daughters of author Iris Origo used to rent out their gorgeous (and massive) apartments to exclusive visitors to Rome, or when the international law firm which owns part of the main floor have been gracious enough to open their rooms and gardens to participants in seminars I have taught.

I point out to visitors that this is probably the oldest inhibited building on the planet. Where else is a building dating back two millennium anything other than a museum or monument?

When Augustus evicted the industry from the Campus Martius it found a new home downriver. In the shadows of the Monte Testaccio landfill were emporia, warehouses, marble cutting yards, and industrial docks. Fittingly centuries later when Rome was chosen capital of newly unified Italy this area was once again designated as the site of what the master plan called the "noisy industries," referring to those facilities necessary to support city life but undesirable in ones own backyard. NIMBY lobbyists in the noble families in central and northern Rome determined that Testaccio and Ostiense would be the sites for the slaughterhouse (1875), the central markets, the gas plants and electrical generation facilities, as well as river ports and train stations. In fact the presence of the river, rail lines and the ancient consular road (Via Ostiense) made this a highly strategic and desirable location. Public housing constructed in Testaccio and nearby Garbatella would provide the necessary manpower, while the great Montemartini generator plant would burn coal and later diesel to provide electrical power.

By the late 20th century the city had once again outgrown its bounds and the edge of town was again engulfed by the growing center. As industry moved elsewhere, abandoned factories were made available for redevelopment. Key to the platform of progressive Mayors Rutelli and Veltroni in the 1990s and early 2000s were programs to reprogram these *industrie dismesse* (abandoned factories) and these same strategies are again on the tables of Mayor Marino's urban transformation team led by Giovanni Caudo.

The most acclaimed urban revitalization in Rome is certainly the transformation of the former Montemartini power plant into an overflow venue for Capitoline Museum collection. Built in the 1912, with several upgrades to its turbines in the 1930s and 1950s, this served as the city's primary power generator until its closure in the 1970s. In the early 1990s I experienced the industrial archaeology of the then-abandoned Montemartini plant as part of an "itinerant" performance of Kafka's *Amerika*, staged by director Giorgio Barberio Corsetti. The play opened on one of the unused platforms of the Ostia Lido train station, moved (by metro) to Garbatella and the Montemartini, and culminated in a bonfire on the banks of the Tiber. The use of the machines of the former power plant as a stage for contemporary art demonstrated once again how the ephemeral can provide a catalyst for urban transformation. About eight years later, in 1997, the *Ex-Centrale Montemartini* was renovated as an experiment and hosted the temporary exhibit "The Machines and the Gods," a display of classical statuary and other finds from Roman excavations which the Capitoline Museum lacked the space to put on display. The critical success of the exhibit from its opening resulted in its extension as a permanent showcase for ancient and industrial archaeology, set off against one another in a poetic and compelling juxtaposition.

The museum's economic failure (averaging just a handful of visitors a day) shouldn't be blamed on the strategic or aesthetic choice but rather on the city's inability to keep tourists, who should be the prime resource for economic growth, for more than a couple of days. The potential for adaptive reuse of industrial archaeology, like the reuse of the ancient Theatre of Marcellus, is thrilling to any visitor who take the time to explore this alternative Rome, beyond the Colosseum and St. Peter's. Sadly, the city today, mired in illegality and marred by blight, repels its visitors while seducing them. After a day or two, tired of dodging cars, waiting for buses that never come, finding museums closed or overcrowded, shocked to see pickpockets and illegal vendors working undisturbed under the nose of the authorities, licking their wounds, many leave frustrated vowing never to return.

Places of Waste

Like many architects, I am in love with simple, minimal elegance, with clean lines and stripped down, ordered space. But I have become increasingly aware of the cost which accompanies minimal design; behind any minimal looking design usually lies an inefficient mess hidden away somewhere, often far away. It is this dialectic of clean space/messy space which we need to recognize in design of any scale, including cities.

At the smallest scale of domestic space, this is the role of closets. In order to have a tidy, slick, minimal interior we do one of several things: 1. strip our lives of most of our objects, something many of us strive for but few really want to achieve, so we do 2. periodically throw the clutter in the trash, and when we need something go out and buy it, unless we are lucky to have sufficient storage space in which case we do 3. store the clutter but keep it nearby for when it might come in handy. Of course, #2 is the least efficient and (if we dismiss #1 as a pipe dream) #3 is by far the best solution. It results in a place that is neither on stage nor discarded; a kind of wings where stuff can wait unobtrusively (a concept I recall as being key to the simplicity of Japanese homes).

I'm a packrat as well as a design snob, which means I fill this kind of middle space (my basement, storage lofts, walk-in closets) with things that I have no use for at present but anticipate some unknown future use.

At the scale of urban space a similar concept applies, but storage of detritus is rarely designed into master plans; it just happens. It fills the gaps alongside railroad tracks, it is tossed into landfills, and at best it shows up at flea markets and junk yards. These places usually go by the label "blight" and urban design seeks to eradicate them, which only serves to raise the cost of waste and the need for consumption. This is not the "Junkspace" Rem Koolhaas extols. It is closer to Alan Berger's concept of Drosscape, "large tracts of abused land on the peripheries of cities and beyond, where urban sprawl meets urban dereliction," which in turn derives from Lars Lerup's use of the term "dross" in contrast to "stim," the stimulating, deliberately developed urban areas.[3] Observations of third world squatter towns provide abundant precedents for the smart use of what we in the first world often dismiss and discard as waste. Scott Brown tells of the Cape Dutch farmhouse she visited in South Africa where the floor was made of cow dung and and peach pits, "seen as valuable resources, not waste, in that society." Enough material exists on the space of waste (not to be confused with the waste of space) to devote entire urban design studios.

But idealizing/romanticizing "dross" is at best unnecessary and at worst pathetic and counterproductive. It should be recognized as useful piece of the urban puzzle, considered and provided but not aestheticized. Of course, the gritty marginal spaces of the city feature prominently in fiction and films— think of Pasolini, Jim Jarmusch, Wim Wenders and countless others— but this is quite different from recreating the aura of abandonment in new design. Michael Benedikt refers to " environmental stoicism," our "ability to tune out places that are cheap, neglected, depressing" but also what he calls "place machismo," the tendency— of architects especially —to find inspiration in the grim embrace of harsh realities such as abandoned factories, gypsy camps, railroad sidings, and the likes.

An architecture which deals appropriately with such space of waste should do so practically and ecologically, with the same approach we use for organic farming. The goal should be to reuse whatever is on a site as close to the site as possible without damaging the health and well-being of the residents, but rather contributing to the on-site economy.

Innovative Reuse

Examples abound of economic phenomena based on innovative reuse. Often the consequence of poverty, many of these occur in the informal economies of the developing world. On the outskirts of Cairo the Zabbaleen, a community of Coptic Christians, collect, sort and process the city's trash, separating out reusable and recyclable waste and, until a 2009 health law forbid it, feeding food scraps to pigs. Slums in general, as Stewart Brand has observed, rely on the adjacency to wealth in order to glean from its waste, a mutually beneficial synergy that is undermined by misplaced attempts at cleaning up the city, like the slaughter of pigs in Cairo. In Rome it is common to see Romani from Eastern Europe rummaging through dumpsters, mining the city's trash for resources. The activist group Stalker-Osservatorio Nomade has recognized the innovative value of this activity and focused a series of workshops on the Romani communities. Such synergies work less well when the global north and global south are kept separate, distanced by space and high security fences, and yet the informal economy thrives even there. Like dark energy in astrophysics, Brand says, "it's not supposed to be there but it is."

In more recent cases, re-use has arisen from a conscious desire to live more sustainably and here too examples using found materials abound, from the Rural Studio projects in Alabama to the Cirque du Soleil headquarters in Montreal, Italian organizations like *Cianfrusoteca* and *Barotopoli*, the Dutch Atelier *Bom Design* and countless others. From an economics of frugality, re-use has now become trendy, not in itself a reason for dismissal. The ethics of environmental awareness has found its match in a green aesthetics. Culture and sustainability, often poised in opposition, have found common ground in old stuff.

Re-use, perhaps even more than other productive activities given its space requirements and low economic value, often takes place in the public realm. The overflow of productive activity into informal public spaces often takes place when growth meets its limits, spatial or economic (usually one and the same). Many productive activities begin by default in the public realm. Hunting and grazing took place in the wilderness and the commons before the enclosure of agricultural lands and game reserves. Selling was itinerant until the establishment of a reliable enough market to support a fixed location. "Place taking" precedes "place making." Businesses usually start on kitchen tables before graduating into purpose built facilities, performing essential innovations in coffee shops and public libraries. Rock bands and high tech start-ups both famously begin in garages and seedy bars, alternatively occupying the extremes of cramped private spaces and vibrant public ones before finding their own, often banal, middle ground in functionally specific containers. These extremes of public and private work together to offer a surprisingly efficient venue for productive work; in my limited private space I store personal things, retreat to privacy, but when I want a change of scene, a breath of fresh air, society, stimulus and open space I bring my laptop out to the piazza or the park.

Especially when work requires space or involves irritating substances moving outside is the best option. From pueblo villages to European medieval towns, craftspeople have often set up temporary workplaces in the public realm.

Throughout Rome, still today tiny workshops spill into the streets in warm weather. These artisans are an endangered species in the late capitalist economy, evicted to make way for fast food, souvenirs, slot machines, internet points and the like, especially in the touristic center of Rome. However, the very existence of blight-ridden, abandoned property in the center of the city may provide the opportunity for survival of an economy which bypasses the cycle of consumption and disposal and instead promotes local, informal productive use of public space and the smart use of information technology.

La Periferia Centrale

One of Rome's most archetypically marginalized sites is at the heart of the city, along the Tiber river, a short walk from the Circus Maximus. For several years the California Polytechnic University Rome Program and other American architecture courses have focused on this site for workshops aimed at proposing an architecture of and for material reuse.

The premise of the workshop was that cities produce waste and consume materials and energy, but this is not necessarily "by nature." Products which today become broken or obsolete are discarded when they could be repaired, reused, regenerated or, as a last resort, see their component materials recycled. Traditionally, such activities have often been marginalized, performed by outcasts in blighted parts of cities. Rome, however, has a tradition of productive workshops in its historical center, now being rapidly forced out of existence by global economics. In an emergent green economy this work will become more appreciated and more central to a mixed use urban ecology.

The university projects called for the transformation of the site of the former papal arsenal at Porta Portese into a Center for Rome's (traditional and emergent) "Green Economy," an urban resource center or a center for material reuse–anything but a "junkyard." The challenge was to create a vibrant place in which urban synergies and efficiencies are maximized, by design, to reduce "waste" to close to zero.

Another goal of the Center is to bring production and commerce back together. It intends to provide workshops to some of those artisans who fix, produce and sell objects, but have been forced to move out or to close down their business. The project brief called for "an area of buildings and open spaces dedicated to the stockpiling, repair, dis-assemblage, reuse and recycling of used technology, from bicycles to computers, including everything but motor vehicles (which require more space and produce more toxins). It would be a place where people can bring things to fix or hack, where someone can drop off a broken washing machine knowing it will be treated as resource, not waste.

Interestingly, many of the projects started with a strongly digital framework, a database of parts and system for cataloging and sorting, observing that often the problem is not "not having" the part but not finding it or recognizing its potential. Sophisti-cated storage systems emerged, resembling libraries or archives more than yard sales. The role of creative arts was held foremost with studio spaces for visual artists and designers who use found materials in innovative ways; many projects integrated design and manufacturing in adjacent spaces.

In all the more successful projects the result was not a closed facility but an open community space including public gardens with agricultural use, integrated with the river's ecosystem. While commerce is present in the projects, as is gastronomy, it is part of a near closed-cycle loop, especially when considering the greater community of Trastevere and Testaccio. In review-ing the outcome of the workshops, the participants and critics observed that the resulting public spaces provided a role for all kinds of knowledge, from the know-how of the old-timer ready to give out technical advice to the open source sharing of sys-tematically catalogued data. By grounding social encounters in material objects, but rejecting the obsessive and ecologically dysfunctional "discarding of the old to make way for the new," more complex relationships are made possible.

Public space is energized by the innovative re-use of materials and plays a productive civic role. Out of this experience came the master plan proposal for the urban makeover of the Porta Portese neighborhood elaborated by my firm, TRA_20, in 2013.

Piazza di Pietra, Rome

Square of Stone

The results of the Cal Poly workshop for Porta Portese were put on display in 2010 in an exhibit entitled Foreign Architects Rome (FAR) at the Temple of Hadrian on Piazza di Pietra, one of the city's most elegant piazzas. The occasion was part of the Festa dell'Architettura and included the work of nine university programs (members of the association AACUPI) and an equal number of architects from the various foreign academies.

A more appropriate venue could not have been chosen to display projects related to adaptive reuse. Originally built in about 140 by Hadrian's adopted son and successor, Antoninus Pius this monument stood tall above the Campus Martius, its 50-foot marble columns surrounding the stone faced *cella* containing a statue to the deified architect-emperor Hadrian, responsible for the Pantheon (just down the street). Over the centuries the temple has seen numerous transformations, acting as Napoleon's offices in the early 19th century, Rome's stock exchange in the mid 20th century, and now, since the 1990s, an exhibition and conference space for Rome's Chamber of Commerce.

Its street address in Piazza di Pietra tells another story, one of material reuse. *Pietra* (stone) was the material available to be quarried from the eroding temple, most likely to be burnt for quicklime in the lime kilns. Appropriately, material reuse was the subject of our students' principle design project, on display along a selection of quotes used to express the issues being addressed and their global-local urgency. Visitors were impressed to see the attention of the international architectural world focused not just on the historical monuments and cultural traditions of Rome, but on the complex urban systems that make any city an effective ecological habitat.

Bridging the Gap

In the 1970s and 80s, when I was in architecture school, after an important but very fleeting burst of environmentalist thinking from the likes of British economist E. F. Schumacher (Small is Beautiful) to American engineer Buckminster Fuller (Spaceship Earth), an interest in history again emerged. People began to recognize the artifacts present in the city as repositories of meaning, rather than obstacles to progress.

For theorists of the post-modern, the value of history was often in its age and its aura, the associations that come with it, not in its actual material. Architecture was so busy trying to look "contextual" or vaunting pithy, mannered, historical references that it ignored its own role in the evolving city, often replacing real history with an ersatz version. Fortunately, little of this marred Italy, although Italian architect Aldo Rossi was one of its (inadvertent) perpetrators.

Instead of reading history as pure meaning to be quoted knowingly (the historians' reading) or as pure material to be recycled (the bricoleur's reading), can architects accept the complexity on both levels, treating urban design as a process of increasing knowledge and performance through critical acts of preservation and urban transformation? Ruskin said "Take proper care of your monuments and you will not need to restore them." For Cesare Brandi the first step in deciding if a work of art is worth preserving is recognition of it as a work of art: the second step is preserving its material support. This distinct yet inseparable quality of aura and tangible composition, of meaning and material, underlies our reading of cities. In fact, Brandi's brand of critical conservation is the basis for the accepted Charter of Preservation.

Jane Jacobs said that "old ideas can sometimes use new buildings[4]. New ideas must come from old buildings." Stewart Brand distinguishes between high road buildings that can't be touched and "low road" ones that are street tough, that you can put a nail into without complaints. Then there are "no road" buildings, or what Brand terms magazine architecture. According to cyberpunk writer William Gibson "the street finds its own uses for things."

The challenge as a designer in a rich and complex urban context (none more so than Rome) is not to compete and to stand out; with exceptions made for temporary exhibits and ephemeral projects of which Rome has a great history, most architecture has consequences that should prohibit it from following fleeting trends of fashion. No one but a few critics and historians will care about how daring or unprecedented a project was after it has been in place for a few decades. Nor should our objective be to embalm the past under glass as if history has ended.

Carl Elefante's observation that the greenest building is one that already exists is a starting point, not an end. I believe we can dialogue with the past, operate on our cities in ways that improve not only our performance, but also our fit. It is not enough to reduce the negative impact of our cities. We have to ensure that our impact is positive and regenerative. It is a design problem in which the architect has the onus of bridging the gap between cultural knowledge and scientific knowledge.

Notes

1. Corsi, Faustino, 1771-1845: *Delle pietre antiche* (Roma : Tipografia Salviucci, 1833)

2. Largo Argentina is now better known for the cat sanctuary which shares the space with the ruins, profiting from the fact that when archaeology is protected its feline inhabitants will also be safe from the risks of modern life.

3. In addition, Kevin Lynch addressed the positive aspects of waste space in his last work "The Waste of Place," and Denise Scott Brown, in a talk called Art of Waste presented at Basurama makes similar observations.

4. Jane Jacobs, *Life and Death of the Great American City*. (Cambridge, MA: M.I.T. Press, 1961)

CHAPTER 6.

TRANSPORTATION: ALL ROADS, THEN AND NOW

Engineer Antonio Tamburrino, who was at the table of the 1972 Club of Rome meeting that resulted in the publication of *The Limits of Growth*, says that the concept of transportation was born in Rome through the creation of roadways[1]. Today Rome is a traffic engineer's nightmare, but at the time of Julius Caesar wheeled traffic was banned from the center of town during daylight hours to reduce traffic.[2]

The simplest, cheapest technologies—buses, light rail, bicycles and other forms of personal transport (Segways, etc.)—hold the most promise as the solutions. However, there are two major caveats to their success: a nearly surgical attention to archaeology and the elimination of private automobiles. Drawing from the ideas and experience of a growing community of experts and activists in Rome and around the world, I'll explain why I'm convinced this can be done.

Rome, Earth

From 10,000 feet in the air, Rome is chaos, a confusing sprawl, denser where the Tiber river straightens and then splits sharply around the Tiber Island, and again denser on the coast. It is hard to perceive the hub and spoke system of the consular roads but the wide ring road, called the GRA, can probably be seen from space.

You don't need a plane to obtain this privileged vantage point, now that satellite data has been made universally available and user friendly. For some people, virtual travel has made real travel redundant. Why go anywhere when information and images of far-away places are pervasive and omnipresent? One obvious reason is for face-to-face contact. But thanks to technology, people can be brought together in ways that virtually eliminates the need for physical travel. For that reason, as well as growing carbon awareness and the fear of terrorism, travel is likely to decline in the years to come.

As travel became increasingly commonplace, places in effect became smaller, and cultural homogeneity began to replace local customs and cultural differences. Visiting Rome in the early 80s still felt like foreign travel; the time, currency, language, food, everything changed. Passing from Greece to Turkey, or from

Egypt to Israel, were radical experiences. I could find products and foods in markets there that didn't exist at home. We can hope that the reduction of physical travel and shipping will once again encourage local cultures to thrive and flourish.

Information, words, pictures and even music all travel pretty well, and Web 2.0, which gives access to them instantly and everywhere, carried this to its logical extreme. Whether I am in a cafe in Istanbul or a library in Amsterdam, the databases I consult are the same. But stuff and people cannot be moved around so easily, especially when we consider the true cost of their mobility. It makes more sense to eat food produced locally, and to inhabit buildings built by local workers with locally materials. While art and literature can travel, their meaning changes depending on context. Reading Joyce in Dublin is more stimulating than reading him in New Delhi or LA. Similarly, eating Chinese food in China is different from eating it in London, even if the food is the same. Simply stated, with a reduction in travel comes a return to local identity; when we do travel the experience is richer, more engulfing.

Walking in Rome

Years ago I founded a travel association, *Scala Reale*, whose members had, for the most part, flown half-way around the globe to explore, on foot, Rome and other Italian towns. They were enthralled with the vibrant and walkable streets, a stark contrast to the suburban American landscapes which most called home. They observed a city conceived for pedestrians but increasingly invaded by automobiles.

The mission of the association was to provide an alternative to both the dumbed-down experience of mass tourism and insulated, as well as isolating, do-it-yourself guidebook travel.

Through on-site talks, walks and seminars, held mostly in English, *Scala Reale* brought together lovers of Roman culture from various backgrounds to explore and unravel the monuments and neighborhoods of Rome. To avoid damaging cultural heritage sites by invading them en-masse, groups were limited to no more than six people at a time. This formula, small enough to function like an intimate in-depth seminar, yet without the exclusivity of privately contracted "guiding," was hugely successful and was later adopted by commercial travel ventures such as Context Travel. *Scala Reale* was a non-profit cultural association, a peculiarly Italian business model under which cultural activities, whether they be lessons or performances or what not, can be organized for the association's members under a simplified fiscal regime. At its height in 2000, it had thousands of members, dozens of whom were actively involved as docents researching and leading itineraries.

Scala Reale took root at the dawn of the Internet and was one of the first organizations to link this new globalized media with the local cultural reality of a specific place. It bridged, on the one side, architects, historians, archaeologists and others with in-depth knowledge of Rome and a knack for communication and, on the other, discerning individuals, thirsty for knowledge about Rome. Together they sought an experience that would go beyond "tourism," for something more akin to a university seminar or museum talk. Enter the internet 1.0, and this link could be made quickly and cheaply, person to person, bypassing middlemen and agencies.

For me, the principal thrill was in the designing of itineraries, and I use the word "design" pointedly. Whereas in designing a building an architect establishes a complex set of enclosures, thresholds, surfaces, voids, vistas and bodily comforts, I found the city of Rome was already rich in all but the last. Rather than add to the city's already lavish physical inventory, I thought it more appropriate to design our experience of the city. The raw material was there but the situations were wrong; instead of leading to enlightenment and passion, interventions were often damaging the very heritage they aimed at displaying. New visitors' centers, new signage, concentrations of tour buses, hightech "infotainment" installations, souvenir outlets, — all of the money and effort was aimed at separating the visitor from the city.

Scala Reale aimed to do the opposite; to design and choreograph itineraries which went against the current. We strolled down shady side streets instead of looking out a bus window on a major boulevard, and stopped to chat with artisans instead of being ushered into merchandise "outlets." Beyond the purely visual or informational aspects of "sightseeing," the itineraries appealed to all the senses: the echoing silence in church, the smells of flowering trees, the taste of coffee, the warmth of a sun-filled piazza on a winter afternoon (or the chill of an underground archaeological site).

Itineraries were designed with seasons and time of day in mind, timed to turn a corner just as the sun illuminated a Baroque facade or as a chanted Latin mass was underway or when hot pizza came out of the ovens. Although planned, the routes were flexible enough to adapt to that inevitable surprise, with docents varying the path in response to unforeseen obstacles or opportunities.

Above all, the itineraries were walks (or occasional bike rides). The problem of mobility was solved in the simplest way possible, on two feet. In central Rome, the area where the vast majority of tourists are concentrated, nothing is further than a brisk 20 minute walk away.[3] In fact, in central Rome, motorized vehicles are more a hindrance than a help, blocking far more movement than they facilitate (as will be discussed below).

Setting out from Piazza del Popolo, you might veer onto Via Margutta, ducking into art galleries and green courtyards, stop for a sip of fresh water bumbling from Pietro Bernini's fountain at the base of the Spanish Steps, window shop along Via Condotti, traverse the Via del Corso past the palaces of the Italian government, grab an espresso at the Tazza D'Oro, pop into the Pantheon, shortcut through the Gothic church of Santa Maria Sopra Minerva past one of Michelangelo's lesser known works, and a few minutes later emerge at the base of the Capitoline Hill. As the crow flies you have covered but one kilometer. The straight route on foot down Via del Corso would have taken you no more than 20 minutes and a bit less in a taxi, but the meandering walk has enriched you in uncountable ways. The first goal of transit policy should be to put more people within an engaging 20 minute walk of their destination.

Typical scenes of urban blight in Rome in 2015

Rome's Automobile Obsession

Passenger cars are responsible for 12 percent of greenhouse gas emissions in Europe — a proportion that is growing, according to the European Environment Agency — and up to 50 percent in some car-intensive areas in the United States. Petroleum now accounts for 97 percent of the energy used in transportation in the US. Intercity mass transit (like trains) uses one-tenth as much fuel per passenger mile as private autos. For intracity transit it is 1/6th.[4]

Italy, a civilization whose origins predate the chariot, let alone Fiat, has one of the highest per capita rates of car ownership on the planet. Among its major cities only one, Catania, is worse than Rome, where for every 100 inhabitants there are 69 cars, over 10 times more than in the 1960s, when there were only six. And it's not just a problem of fossil fuel consumption and emissions. In Italy motor vehicles inflict a startling human cost: there are 27 traffic accidents every hour, mortalities from accidents are about one an hour, and an average of two pedestrians die in Italy each day. The cost of Rome's cultural addiction to automobiles extends to all aspects of life in the capital. It fuels the inefficiencies of what is otherwise a strong health-care system, bogged down with car-related injuries. It dominates the use of real estate which could otherwise be put to more productive uses. It mars the cityscape and landscape, Rome's most precious asset for the tourist economy. It is so obvious a problem that it is shocking that so many Romans seem either oblivious or resigned to accept it.

Officials talk about how complicated Rome is, but it's often quite simple. There are cars where there shouldn't be cars: in pedestrian zones, on sidewalks, in crosswalks, at bus stops and blocking scooter parking areas. American tourists find the tiny microcars and Smart cars endearing, and may see them as signs of environmental concern, but more and more the streets are cluttered with oversized SUVs out of scale with a city like Rome.

On my daily bike or scooter commute from Monteverde to Circus Maximus I can usually count hundreds of cars in no parking zones (and fines are so rare as to make the practice cost-effective). I can't help but ask the obvious, questions that may seem incomprehensible in this culture so firmly enslaved to the car.

1. If all the cars parked in violation of city laws were to pay the fines (for laws already on the books) how much money would enter the city's coffers? Certainly enough to cover some additional law enforcement personnel, improvements to public trans-

portation and enough left over for bike paths. Not to mention that many people who drive now knowing they can park illegally without risk would consider other options. So why doesn't this happen?

2. What if parking in Rome cost what it does in other cities, like New York ($40/day average) instead of €4/day? Again, how much money could be used for essential public services and how many fewer cars would we see clogging the roads, consuming fuel and polluting the air? The value of the 10 square meters of city land taken up by a parking space alone, without even considering the cost of maintenance, should be about €600/month or €20/day, so why does the city give it away for €1/hour?

3. Italy, a relatively small country, has more government vehicles–mostly top-of-the-line luxury cars—than the United States. Really, where is it written that politicians and bureaucrats need to drive to work at taxpayers' expense? Why doesn't the government sell most of these and let the politicians walk or ride the bus?

4. Even when civil servants don't have government-issued cars, they still expect to have parking provided at their place of work in the city. Why do public employees get to drive to work? Professors, doctors and architects and thousands of other professionals find their own solution to the daily commute, but the civil servants who we pay to keep our society together can't. It's common even to see cars branded with ATAC, the public transit agency, driving around town. This city would work a lot better if its managers and law enforcers were out riding the buses and walking the streets.

5. One reason Rome's municipal police rarely issues tickets to illegally parked cars (even when they are standing right next to

them) is that they are too busy "directing traffic" at crowded intersections, duplicating the job of the traffic light with the justification that there are so many cars that they would create gridlock without police intervention. What if they just let the gridlock happen and fined the cars that entered the intersection without being able to reach the other side before the light changes? More money for the city, less incentive for drivers.

6. The last is my current pet peeve: why are there advertisements for cars on public buses? In fact, why isn't it illegal to advertise automobiles period, given their clear threat to public health, and their role in the destruction of our cities? Car ads on buses are like cigarette ads on ambulances.

The list could go on, but the problem is quite simple. The real culprit is the incentives for private auto use and the disincentives for other forms of transportation. Bike sharing, car sharing are palliative measures, not intended to really replace cars but rather to "brand" the city administration as green.[5]

Recent purchases of "clean" electric cars by Rome's administration further fuel the auto industry but keep the city from confronting its auto addiction. Only when Romans get over this love affair with the car, and see these machines as out of place in the city as an elephant in a china shop, will Rome again become a truly green city.

I'm convinced that the simplest solution lies in simply enforcing the existing laws regarding motor vehicles. Despite a relatively high 50km/h speed limit throughout the city (London has lowered its to 30), a few years ago cars could be clocked at double this on Via Fori Imperiali near the Colosseum. This road, where a young cyclist was killed several years ago, is now almost car-free with the exception of occasional government cars whose speed negates the whole idea of a safe haven for pedestrians.

Despite parking restrictions typical of most European cities, autos can be seen everywhere in violation and rarely fined. This has been long accepted as sign of Italy's famous flexibility with regard to the law, turning a blind eye to minor violations. But urban residents are starting to get fed up. I work with a number of pedestrian advocacy groups and public space planners and, thanks especially to the web and to blogs like my own, initiatives to fight the automotive addiction are growing. Fed up with the lack of enforcement of parking laws we have started distributing our own symbolic citizen's fines, attempting to sensitize drivers to the fact that their personal convenience comes at the price of the rights and safety of hundreds of pedestrians and cyclists, children and elderly, people who are consuming no fossil fuels and producing no emissions.

Our goal is to shift the balance back to a mix of public transit and walking/cycling. Rome's public transit network, in particular its buses and light rail, is potentially one of Europe's best, were in not for the congestion of private vehicles and inconsistent management. Given a choice of a clean, efficient transit system and pleasant safe streets for walking and cycling, reinforced by costly and rigorously enforced parking restrictions, most Romans will eventually overcome their automobile addiction.

Elsewhere in Italy

The most innovative transit systems I've experienced are in large Italian airports and small Italian cities. When I studied Italian, I lived in the Umbrian capital Perugia, a dense, medium-sized city perched on the top of a steep ridge. At the time, one could reach the center of town by elevator, passing first through a long tunnel under the hillside, or by a space-age escalator system that ascended through caves and then the basement of a 19th century palace. One moment you were at the edge of town, on wide streets with cars and modern buildings, and the next you were in narrow stone streets with few motor vehicle in sight. I thought of this conveyer system like walking through the wardrobe into Narnia, or being beamed from the Starship Enterprise to a medieval space station.

On a recent trip to Perugia, for Italy's *Festa dell'Architettura*, I check out the city's newest and even more futuristic transit revolution, the Mini-Metro. Essentially a monorail, on (red) tracks spanning valleys or buried under the medieval town, it is automatic, silent and beautiful. The design is distinctive — French architect Jean Nouvel was called in to design the stations — but the technology is that of ski-lifts and airport conveyers. My son and I parked our car in an efficient new parking structure by the old train station, and entered the steel and glass mini-metro station with its razor-thin roof shading sleek transparent walls. The little red shuttle arrived within minutes and swooshed us (and about a dozen others) on a roller-coaster ride above rooftops of houses and through the treetops before disappearing into winding tunnels through the hill on which the old city stands. A few stops later, we hopped off, a bit disoriented as we emerged by escalator into a square in the heart of town.

We were not far from the University for Foreigners, where years ago I studied Italian. When I lived here, my commute to school took me along the top of a medieval aqueduct, reconditioned as a pedestrian walkway. The experience was similar, using light, highly crafted infrastructure to move from outside to in, and the concept is the same whether the flow is of people, water, electricity or what have you. What do the locals think of this addition to the historic urban landscape? As often is the case, the project was met with as many complaints as compliments, especially suggestions that the money would have been better spent fixing the roads!

Skytrain

The technological solutions to movement in medieval Perugia recall a very different setting: the sky-train at Rome's Fiumicino airport, which brings passengers to Terminal D. It inspired me to imagine something similar in downtown Rome. An automated, driverless, shuttle zips its passengers between two points. Only one track is needed, widening in the middle where the vehicles pass. The logic is that of a horizontal elevator. Imagine one between Piazza del Popolo and Piazza Venezia, and between Piazza Venezia and the Colosseum, or from Castel Sant'Angelo to St. Peters. Of course, the alternative of a fascinating 20 minute walk or 5 minute bike ride makes such futuristic infrastructure a lower priority.

Except when there are hills. Many cities with hills (Naples, Paris, and Barcelona, to name a few) use funiculars to connect different elevations within the city. The concept is similar—a single track, driverless trains, etc.— but the value to the user (at least those going up) is huge. In Rome I live in Monteverde, at the top of the Janiculum Hill, and usually use a bike to get around. Of course the ride down is fantastic but on my way up the hill I have been known to get off and walk, or squeeze my folding bike onto a public bus. A project by Mario Maniera Elia and Carlo Gasparrini proposed a simple two-car transit solution which, if financed and built, would revolutionize the connection to the hilltop park and the neighborhood beyond. Passing from near the river's edge, up alongside the boundary of the Botanical Gardens, the funicular would allow city dwellers to easily, quickly and quietly reach the parks with their clean air and green space, but it would also serve the residents of the populous Monteverde quarter, providing a more dependable connection to the historic center then the private automobiles and scooters — or the broken down and infrequent buses—used today.

Funiculars were a fixture in many modern cities and unlike trams, which were often dismantled to free up streets for cars, they have continued to provide transit. Some connect inhabited quarters; the *funiculare* in Naples from the Spanish Quarter to Vomero or in Paris the Montmartre *funiculeur* are just some examples. Others connect to natural sites like the Barcelona Parc de Montjuic or Bilbao Artxanda, effectively bringing the countryside closer to the city.

Venice's Grand Canal

Car-free in the Lagoon

Every fixed, reliable structured transit solution, whether an elevator or escalator, a funicular or a tram or a mini-metro, has the potential to reduce the invasion of private cars in our cities. In Venice the *vaporetto*, or public boat, has this effect (assisted by the physical impossibility for cars to circulate)!

When I go to Venice, usually for the architecture Biennale with students in tow, I buy a 2 or 3 day pass which allows unlimited rides on the *vaporetti*. I have learned the routes that get from island to island — the city is nothing more than a cluster of 118 islands — or simply from one side of the Grand Canal to the other. With only six bridges, the canal still poses a significant barrier, one that is also breached by the *traghetti*, traditional gondolas requisitioned as public transit.

One morning we leave our hotel in the Canareggio (former Jewish ghetto), too early for the cruise ships to have discharged their load of daytrippers. The "streets" along the canal are filled with children walking to school, shopkeepers opening their shutters, merchants setting up stands. We walk across a bridge, down an alley, left, then right, then left through a narrow street. Dead ended in a courtyard, we backtrack. We hit water but instead of another dead end, this time we climb onto the tippy black gondola and stand as it pushes off across the canal toward the markets of Rialto. This San Toma' *traghetto* crossing is one of the seven that shuttle commuters across the canal (€2 euros for tourists, 50 cents for locals). At the other side we are in the middle of the bustling market, where the former president of the fisherman's association talks to my students about the Adriatic maritime ecosystem and its effect on the fish market. Boats tied to the pier unload sea bass, mussels, oysters, mackerel and other seafood.

The next boat we board is the Number 1 *vaporetto* which chugs into the Rialto dock where its skilled skipper and crew go through the procedure they repeat hundreds of times a day at the 22 some odd stops on the route. We sweep our passes in front of the ticket reader and join waiting passengers at the floating "bus stop" just as the boat sidles up to the dock its engines pushing to slow its momentum. The deck hand throws big lines around iron bollards and then slides the steel gate aside to allow passengers to discharge. When the last elderly Venetian with her shopping cart has stepped off the boat, it is our turn to board (in an orderly fashion that I can't imagine in Rome). This boat will take us on a magical voyage through a landscape right out of Canaletto, past San Marco and the Doge's Palace, out into the lagoon to our destination, the Arsenale of the Venetian Navy, where cutting-edge architectural projects from around the world are on display at the Biennale.

Standing on the deck, I note that the only other motorized vehicles one sees (all water borne) are used for delivery, emergency or taxis. A bureaucrat in Venice doesn't drive a boat to work, a shopkeeper doesn't double-park a boat outside her shop, and even smartly dressed lawyers hop a *vaporetto* and walk to their final destination without sacrificing status or social standing. The density of people is as astounding as is the variety of use; children playing, students stopping to chat, merchants selling wares, business people moving quickly to destinations, all coexist.

Venice cannot be held up as an example of the ideal city; its population has dropped drastically in recent decades and clearly there are reasons beside the reckless real-estate policies which encouraged the exodus. Yet on a purely experiential level, a few days spent in such a humane urban environment remind me that we can do much better than what we settle for in Rome. Water or not, the situation in Rome should be the same; few private vehicles clogging the arteries, leaving space for efficient buses and trams, pleasant public space for pedestrians and bikers, safety for children and the elderly, and a better future for the planet.

Holland

From Venice let's pass on to Amsterdam, another city built on water. It is midsummer and I am on a long-awaited reconnaissance mission to northern Europe, to cities that have a reputation for livability and sustainability that Rome can no longer claim. In fact, this trip was bookended by a transit strike the day of departure (resulting in massive delays, confusion, stress and expense) and another potential transit disaster upon my return caused by a fire at Tiburtina Station, which shuts down much of central Italy's train system. These problems seemed to be accepted with resignation and little information, absorbed like a bout of bad weather. For most Romans, those who dismiss transit as a necessary evil used by immigrants and poor people, the strike had little effect. Even traffic was no worse than usual, since people who have the option of driving seem to exercise that option, strike or no strike.

But, for those who expected transit to work as promised during the hours before the strike, or those tourists who don't understand Italian, it was disastrous. At Terracina station there was no sign, no announcement (in any language) to avert travelers that trains were not running. I encountered a flabbergasted family from Norway who were completely caught off guard and unsure of how to get to Rome's airport to return home[6] In other countries, they said, if a strike is called it is well-publicized in advance in order to call attention to the demands and grievances.

From the air over Milan, I see the healthy model of Italian urbanism, clusters of settlements on hilltops with fields in between, gradually giving way to a dysfunctional model where fields have been "planted" not with food but with cement, sprawling low-density extensions of housing interspersed with the occasional office park, factory or shopping mall.

By contrast, transit in Holland not only works well, but it is well-used. At Schiphol Airport there is a bonafide train station with frequent, economic trains to the center of town. Once there, one is confronted with two smart options: walk (or rent a bike) to reach destinations in the pedestrian friendly center, or hop on transit (metro/tram/bus) to go further afield. Cars exist but are a rarity, like an old-fashioned, nostalgic presence amidst more efficient modes of transportation.

Despite cold and rainy weather, I was able to explore the neighborhoods that interested me, especially Zeeberg and Ijberg, new mixed-use developments on formerly industrial (or formerly non-existent) islands, but also projects from the early 20th century in Rotterdam and Amsterdam, projects where urbanism of a human scale made space for semi-public activities and abundant green space. I saw much new construction, but unlike Rome, where architects are often absent (despite a surplus of them) here the hand of designers was ever-present. Actually, planners and residents as well as designers, because on deeper investigation it was clear that questions of infrastructure, water, waste, energy and effective land-use had been addressed in depth, through community involvement and interdisciplinary brainstorming, long before buildings began to emerge. Although neighborhoods like Ijberg were clearly still under construction, the transit system was fully functional, a high-speed tram/train which went underwater at one point making the connection from the central station to the tip of the new island. I had seen a documentary about the Borneo-Sporenburg project that explained the rationale behind the planning by West 8, and on visiting the site it seemed a great success.

Rome is not Amsterdam, but there are lessons to be learned. Both cultures share a sense of flexibility; in Holland it has been embraced in the form of liberal, but carefully enforced regulations, while in Italy it involves strong but weakly enforced regulations. In Holland clearly people were free to enjoy city life without compromising others, while Rome still suffers from the privileging of the automobile at the expense of its human master.

Barcelona and Bilbao

You don't need to look to the wealthy countries of northern Europe for examples of functioning and equitable urban mobility: on recent trips to Spain I witnessed solutions that progressive city administrators put into place over the past two or three decades.

These cities are famous for architectural landmarks which brought international attention (and, with a clear strategy, global investments); Barcelona learned to leverage its late 19th century archistar, Antonio Gaudi' and Bilbao invited a late 20th century starchitect, Frank Gehry to design the new Guggenheim. Barcelona also commissioned an enormous number of new buildings for the 1990 Olympics and 2004 Barcelona Forum—it would almost be easier to list the architects who haven't left their mark on the city— while Bilbao has continued to bring names like Moneo, Siza, Isosaki and other well-known architects. But in neither case was the presence of architecture as a magnet sufficient to restart the stagnant urban/regional economies.

In Barcelona, the *Barrio Gotico* and nearby Raval were both opened to pedestrians — I prefer this to saying closed to cars — by limiting auto use almost entirely. A small number of underground parking structures, accessible off of larger boulevards at the fringes of the pedestrian zones ensure that there are no cars cluttering the city streets and squares (an almost eery contrast to the sea of metal you see in Rome). These serve a limited number of users who pay market rate for the space they occupy. The developers contracted to construct and manage the parking, in return for the concession, produce and maintain public facilities above.

A small number of Barcelona residents own cars and even fewer use them on a daily basis. A clean and efficient transit system, an extensive and well-managed bike-sharing program, and safe and attractive streets for walking and biking make car use the least attractive mobility option. Like many smart mayors around the world, from London to Bogotá, Barcelona's Pasqual Maragall i Mira simultaneously worked to encourage green mobility and discourage the use of private autos.

The recent transformation of Barcelona into a pedestrian-friendly city provides further scientific evidence to support the hypothesis presented by Jane Jacobs when battling to protect Greenwich Village from Robert Moses. Refuting the unfounded assumptions of traffic engineers, who said that if you close streets to traffic the traffic just goes elsewhere, she proved that if you block vehicular access the vehicles just go away. In Barcelona and any other city where I have seen the lanes open to private traffic reduced to a minimum, accompanied by strict enforcement and a strategy for transit, biking and pedestrian equity, the private cars no longer present a threat. There was some resistance at first by shopkeepers who imagined that fewer cars would mean fewer sales although all evidence points to the contrary. Watching the throngs of tourists and locals with shopping bags crowding the narrow streets in central Raval, I doubt there is much nostalgia for the automobile.

In Bilbao, a much smaller city but still with a center the size of Rome's, my son and I rented bikes and used the bike trails to explore most of the city. When we had to share streets with cars, the traffic was minimal and the speeds civilized. When we wanted to go further afield, such as a trip to the coast, the metro and regional trains ran on schedule and were maintained with dignity. It's not surprising that tourists stay longer in Bilbao than they do in Rome.

Via Appia

Back in Rome, I am on the oldest road in the city, if not the world. The wheels of my bike bounce over the rough basalt paving stones of the Appian Way as I head for the Alban Hills. It is the longest ride I've done in a while, and my legs are hurting, but it is nevertheless a fantastic experience. Thanks are due to Roman politician Appio Claudio for making the road in the 4th century BCE, to Luigi Canina for preserving it as a park in the 19th century, and to the Parco Regionale dell'Appia Antica for maintaining it today.

In 2000 I took travel-writer Rick Steves biking out here for his Rome episode and since then have seen interest in the road and its park grow, with good reason. It's one of Rome's most impressive green archaeology sites.

Today my goal is the Grande Raccordo Annulare, or GRA, the road that rings the city. The last time I really explored the outer reaches of the Appian Way it was still bisected by this high-speed artery, but some years back the GRA was buried to allow the ancient road to continue uninterrupted on its course towards Capua, Benevento and then Brindisi. The GRA has become less of an edge now and more of a connector and cultural icon; the 2013 film *Sacro GRA* sheds light on the strange culture that exists around its fringes. I am interested to find that point where the two iconic roadways overlap.

The light is fantastic and the temperature just right, chilly enough to make the effort of biking pay off in warmth. The first big climb after leaving the gates is a detour through the pastures above (literally) the catacombs of San Callisto, where sheep are grazing on the greenest of grass. I fill up my water bottle at the public fountain and then bike on past the Mausoleum of Cecilia Metella, stopping for a coffee at the bar (which also rents bikes), on to where the road gets bumpy with its ancient basalt blocks, past tombs and statuary. Other than a few other cyclists and joggers (and maybe one car), it is quiet.

Road-based transportation began here in Rome on the Appian Way, the first "highway" in the world, and continued to grow along a dozen consular roads which connected the capital to its provinces. Prior to the creation of such roads travelling between settled areas meant embarking on an adventure with little guarantee of arrival. With the advent of roads transportation became systematized and dependable: all the roads led to Rome which meant Rome was accessible to all. It is true that the roads were designed primarily for pedestrians, but mobility is not so much the question of the mode (foot, animal, wheel) but of the infrastructure (field, network, path, etc.).

As I bike, I reflect on how this great road paved the way for the network of intercity highways that spans continents today. Unlike those toxic arteries, this one is idyllic in its pastoral calm.

In truth, the Appian Way was scaled for people (Roman legions) and not machines, and still today anything bigger than a bicycle is out of place on it. The Appian Way allowed occasional movement of individuals or groups across great distances, but was not made for pointless travel between "non-place" destinations as so many motorways are today. Most trips were still local, on foot, between places well situated in dense city centers.

Reaching the Villa dei Quintilli I know I am near the GRA, my final destination, and I pedal on along what is for me unexplored terrain. And on and on. Can it really be this far? I see airplanes landing and realize I'm near Ciampino airport, which I know is farther out than the GRA. I check the GPS on my phone. Yes, indeed, I have biked right over the multilane high-speed road, as unaware of it as most people are of the catacombs beneath the road closer to Rome. So I turn around and backtrack until the GPS tells me I am right above the highway. Now I notice the telltale signs of bulldozed earth and young trees, but the road has been rebuilt pretty seamlessly where a few years ago it was severed in two. I wish the engineers had left more visible traces instead of consciously burying the modern infrastructure the way time often buries ancient infrastructure.

Nearby the arches of the Acqua Appia aqueduct parade across a field above grazing sheep, a scene which says a lot about the city dweller's need for water, food and clothing, as the ancient Roman road speaks clearly of our need for interconnection. Perhaps by burying our own roads, waterlines, sewers and other infrastructure we lose the clarity that civilizations once had. When our systems are less legible, so is their impact on our lives and our planet.

With that thought, I head back towards Circus Maximus, which

I reach, exhausted, just in time to shop for produce at the weekend Farmers' Market.

Intermodal Solutions

"The streets of Rome are not designed for motor vehicles" is a common observation I hear from tourists and Romans alike, looking for explanations for the congestion of cars in the city. Of course, the narrow streets of the historic center are unsuitable for large vehicles of any sort. Even in ancient Rome wheeled vehicles were banned from the city center during the day to leave space for people. With few exceptions, most of the streets within the Aurelian Walls would be better limited only to pedestrians and bicycles and, okay, the occasional Vespa (but only when driven with skill and respect by a stylish Roman in sunglasses and designer shoes!). But Rome extends far beyond the cliches of tourists and romantics; most of the city is comprised of relatively wide, modern streets, suitable to a wide range of uses.

Whatever the transit mode it must be part of an integrated multimodal system and Rome's road network has spent centuries developing infrastructure for those purposes. People who claim public transit is not suited to Rome should remember that in the mid-20th century the city boasted a strong culture of public transit, visible in the films of neo-realist directors such as Vittorio De Sica or Roberto Rossellini. In De Sica's *The Bicycle Thief* we see trams and buses and bicycles, and people walking in and across streets; the car, a more recent deviation, is practically non-existent in these early films. Bus lines like the *circolare* or trams on the Lungotevere moved through the city with potential regularity not because the government was better organized—there is no evidence that Mussolini "made the trains run on time"— but because there were fewer private automobiles clogging the city's arteries. Rome's streets are perfectly well-suited to public motorized transit and cities like Bogota have shown that by freeing the streets of cars a "bus rapid transit" system can run as smoothly as any underground metro at a fraction of the cost.

Busses and trams do not need to be nostalgic or retrograde. The Phileas system in Eindhoven uses electromagnetic traction and fuel cells, the trams in Bilbao run through regular streets as well as special tracks. They are central to a "smart city strategy."

In the design of Masdar, Foster and Arup insisted that every destination must be easily reachable on foot (150 meters) or bike/segway (500 meters) and designed the Personal Rail Transit system, a network of automated driverless vehicles, to ensure this. Seeing the automobile as a historic relic, William Mitchell set about to reinvent the wheel, making electric cars part of a ubiquitous system tied to a distributed electrical grid as iPods are to iTunes. Cars, for Mitchell, could serve as load levelers, storing excess energy to tap off of during peak hours. Computer networks coordinate transit and energy needs, enabling synergies that couldn't otherwise exist.

It is not cultural heritage or topography that stand in the way of making Rome a more livable city. The notion that Rome's archeological layers make the city incompatible with underground transit, is unfounded. As long as tunnels are deep enough and structurally sound they present no interference. The stations, on the other hand, must penetrate ground rich in ruins, a design challenge which requires precision and care but also offers an unprecedented opportunity to exhibit the city's past in structures outside of the traditional museum.

The underground Metro came to Rome late and with outdated technology, heavy rail identical to that of New York or Paris a century earlier. According to Roman engineer Antonio Tamburrino, an expert on sustainable mobility (and author of the report "*L'orizzonte strategico*") there is a better alternative to the heavy train technology of the Metro C (currently under construction, over budget and unlikely to ever see completion). His "5 rings" proposal calls for trackless trams (running on rubber tires but with an automated magnetic guide), providing a ring of access to parts of the city not currently served by reliable transit (metro or trams). The inner two rings run around the city center, in part below ground and below the archaeological layer. The automated cars would carry a small number of passengers at a high frequency, so a load equal to that of a heavy traditional metro would require only small stations with a minimum footprint.

Bike Planning

Another tired explanation, that a city built on seven hills is no place for bicycles, is being refuted by the increasing presence of cyclists of all ages and social classes in the eternal city. The hills are tiny relative to the expanse of Rome, most of which sprawls out across the Tiber delta. Like the misconception about streets, the challenge to cyclists lies not with the hills but with the traffic that makes biking unhealthy, life-threatening and not very pleasant. Once a month the impromptu Critical Mass brings thousands of bikes together and they "become the traffic." I occasionally attend, although I'm not a fan of the militant scofflaw attitude of some participants. The great thing about Critical Mass is the experience of riding around Rome without a) breathing fumes, b) being deafened by engine noise and c) risking being hit by motor vehicles. Occasionally I've had this same experience when streets have been closed to traffic for special events or emergencies, but until Rome wakes up to the fact that car-free streets are better for everyone the only chance to briefly experience this bliss once a month or so is through militant biking. If that means ticking off a few drivers, so be it.[7]

A few years ago, during the Alemanno administration, I was at the Campidoglio for the presentation of Rome's *Piano Quadro della Ciclabilità*, the plan to promote and support bicycling as an alternative to motorized transport. I went with hopes of seeing tangible proposals that would allow the city to catch up with many of its northern sister cities, where biking is the preferred mode of transit for many.

This was also international "Bike to Work day," although I saw little evidence of it. I saw, as always, at least about 150 cars blocking streets, double-parked, parked on sidewalks, on crosswalks, forcing bikers and pedestrians to weave through traffic. Yet when I arrived at the Campidoglio and locked my bicycle to a pole (at the time there were no bike-racks for the municipal offices) I was immediately approached by police instructing me (with typical Roman courtesy) to park elsewhere.

Critical Mass cycling flash mob in Rome

The Piano Quadro della Ciclabilita' presentation was little more than an opportunity for politicians to make claims of environmental sensitivity. Much of what was said about the advantages of urban cycling, the problems of street safety and the opportunities for the green economy was perfectly valid, but also gratuitous when the administration's responsibility is to solve the problems, not point them out. The cyclists in the audience were visibly and understandably angered at being used instrumentally by politicians, ready for photo opportunities of them "participating" with "citizen groups." As always, the conference began late, the environmental commissioner announcing he would arrive later, no sign of the mayor, and after two hours it was clear that the debate with associations would be cut short or eliminated entirely. I had to leave, frustrated at having heard nothing concrete.

What did I expect? Nothing more. What could I have hoped for?

- Commitment to enforce traffic laws, fining and removing from circulation cars parked illegally, documenting speeding violations, telephone use, etc. etc. including violations by state officials (my collection of documentation of Rome's police committing such infractions is exhaustive). This alone would make the streets of Rome significantly safer without the cost and delay of creating bike paths. And it doesn't require approving any legislation; just enforcing the legislation already on the books. Yes, it's absurd we have to even mention this, but in Rome enforcing the laws is at best an optional.

- Creation of Zone 30 (30 Km/hour zone) throughout the historical center and in specific streets around Rome. Statistically, the mortality rate would drop dramatically. Strange that Maurizio Coppo, head of the national street safety council didn't even mention the concept, common throughout Europe, as a solution.

- Creation of bike racks throughout the city, such as outside the city offices, schools, commercial areas, etc. The claims made by the city about accomplishments in this area are laughable to say the least.

- A city law allowing bike parking in condominium courtyards; this had been mentioned in the press but seems to have dropped out of the law as proposed.

- Clear intermodal transit exchange rules allowing bikes on the Metro and trains all the time, everyday, with improvements to service to make this effectively possible.

- Creation of a bike-sharing program. The one that is constantly held up as a symbol of Rome's green credentials is nothing more than another bike rental agency, not nearly as efficient as dozens that have existed for years.

- And if they want to extend bike paths, that's fine too, but show us the money!

As I left the conference and went to retrieve my bike, locked to a fence out of the way on the edge of the Capitoline hill I pass another "event," the inauguration of the Smart (brand) electric car. There it was, parked in all its glory in the pedestrian zone of Michelangelo's Campidoglio square, where hours earlier I was told to remove my bicycle. This may be as close to the green economy as Rome can get, still holding on to the myth of the car as the only respectable form of transportation, now under the alibi of "zero emissions" (and the electricity is produced by what 100 percent renewable source, *scusi*?) This is where the mayor was, not at the presentation of the cycle plan but at the presentation of another lethal weapon ready to enter Rome's traffic jam.

Dreaming a Different Dream

The solutions seem so obvious to me that I have repeatedly listed them on letters to each mayor, though I am not surprised when I receive no answer (no one ever does in Italy). It's easy to imagine a better Rome, but harder to imagine getting past the administrative and cultural obstacles to achieve it. I'm convinced it's possible and that a day in the city in 2030 might go like this.

You leave your apartment in the working-class Primavalle neighborhood at 8:00 am to head for your office at the city hall. If it's a nice day and you want the exercise you might take your bike; the protected bike trail along the Via Boccea, and down past the Vatican, will get you there in about 20 minutes. If you do this you might leave early to have time to work out and shower at one of the the public gyms with which most workplaces have conventions. But it's rainy and you need to catch up on your email so you walk a few blocks through the green and car-free streets and grab the 8:07 tram which will zip you down to Piazza Venezia in a half-hour in comfort. Taking advantage of the tram's free wifi you work on your laptop and catch up on the news. The tram is not crowded — its automated software guarantees a frequency of 4 minutes — but passengers ascend and descend at each stop: tourists, students, professionals, people of all classes and all ages. As you near your destination in the city center, out the tram window you see lots of bikes and pedestrians and the occasional automobile (taxis and delivery vehicles and a classic Fiat 500 that gives rides to tourists). Descending into Piazza Venezia you stroll across the fast open space bustling with pedestrians sharing space with a few faster moving vehicles which patiently wade their way through the crowd. You are within a 20 minute walk of countless artistic treasures and monuments, privileged to walk the last 10 minutes to your destination along the most beautiful streets in the world.

This vision of a more transit-friendly city doesn't require a major investment — the bike lanes are cheap and much of the tram line already exists — but rather a change of priorities and perspective. The payoff is huge, to residents for whom daily stress of commutes has become intolerable, and to tourists who will stay longer in a car-free city. A more diversified and efficient transit system, coupled with the elimination of private cars from the city center, thus removing the major obstacle to Rome's cultural economy, will mean safer streets for people. And people, after all, are the main participants in the life of the city.

Notes

1. For further information see the video interviews with Tamburrino

which I produced at https://www.youtube.com/
watch?v=5eumOLhT_Kc

2. Ray Lawrence's book The Roads of Roman Italy (London and New York: Routledge, 1999) presents a detailed study of the role of mobility in economic power and cultural change in ancient Rome.

3. "Proximity power," to use Jeremy Rifkin's term, defeats the need for other forms of transport. See Jeremy Rifkin, *The Hydrogen Economy*, (New York: Jeremy P Tarcher. 2004)

4. John Tillman Lyle, *Regenerative Design for Sustainable Development*, (New York: John Wiley and Sons, Inc. 1994), 77.

5. We hear a lot about the Traffic Emergency, but when we look at the details the solutions are often the creation of parking structures, the widening of streets, drafting of new laws to help traffic flow, attracting further vehicles rather than discouraging them.

6. This was the same day a neo-right shooter killed 77 people in Norway, but they didn't yet know about this tragedy.

7. In anticipation of the objections of motorists who "have nothing against bikers but just want to get home" I'm always amazed how the consequences of cars can be so easily ignored. For more on this see https://sustainablerome.wordpress.com/2011/05/30/critical-mass-rome/

CHAPTER 7.

COMMUNITY: SPQR-STYLE

Blue *polizia* vans are wedged into the intersection of two streets near the Pantheon and a wall of young Italian men in riot gear form a wall to keep demonstrators—or anyone else— from reaching Piazza Montecitorio, seat of Italy's Parliament. No protesters are in sight, though, and confused tourists on their way to the Spanish Steps hesitantly ask what is going on and how to get around. How to explain that, behind the closed doors of a Baroque palazzo by Bernini, Italy's government is voting on a law to provide criminal immunity to the prime minister, and the state police have preemptively responded to the threat of protest by putting up a "zona rossa" or security perimeter.

I have seen these red zones pop up around the city and beyond frequently over the years. Sometimes it is in response to natural calamities like the 2009 earthquake in l'Aquila; years later the historic center was still declared off-limits and surrounded by military checkpoints. Other times the barriers go up for special athletic or cultural events, the Rome marathon, a Papal canonization, or a concert. For weeks last summer the public park outside my studio, the site of the ancient Circus Maximus, was closed to the public to set up the stage and support for a mega-concert by the Rolling Stones. The night of the concert a kilometer wide perimeter was set-up and only ticket-holders and residents were allowed through. (I was able to convince the private security that I needed to retrieve my hard-drive from my office and paused to watch Mick Jagger prancing around outside my window.)

Ironically it is often the threat of public participation in public spaces which prompts their closure to the public. Organized protests against government policies or global powers such as the G8 meetings draw massive participation which is framed by authorities as a threat to security. In turn the heavy military turnout is perceived as a challenge to the protesters, mutual taunting turns to street violence and vandalism. The media, traditional and social, fans the flames with its live-tweeting from the war zone and photos of baton-wielding police lobbing tear gas into crowds of angry youth.

Sensationalism Sells

As we know, sensationalism sells and reports of rioting translated into millions of hits on the news sites, where pictures of burning cars and smashed windows shared screen space with ads for new cars and banks and consumer products. When this happens it's hard not to question where the responsibility lies.

Is this really the outcome of pure pent-up rage? The anger is understandable, but I thought those demonstrating were smarter and would avoid falling into the trap of spiraling violence which always plays right into the hand of the forces of repression.

Or is this violence perhaps instigated by those very forces of repression? Our gut response to such a suggestion–"come on, don't be ridiculous," or, in Italian, "ma, ti pare?"– goes a long way toward explaining just why it would be so effective. Burn a few cars and beat a few underpaid cops and you 1. discredit what is starting to emerge as a truly global uprising on the part of 99 percent of humanity, (no, not just a few hippies) 2. justify, in the name of public safety, repression of free-expression by those 99 percent and 3. give a boost to the media and the advertising which now pays its bills. The violence that breaks out in Rome ever more frequently is typical of the old economy where destruction of property, just like wars, diseases and natural disasters, actually show up on balance sheets as positive events because they increase consumption and spending.

Spaces of Democracy

Fortunately, in today's *piazza* — and today's network — the truth tends to surface. At one such clash outside Italy's Senate police were actually filmed "coordinating" with "protestors" on first name basis, and the film with allegations of infiltration rapidly went viral.

Public space (what Richard Sennett called "democratic space") which has its greatest manifestations in the *piazze* of Italian cities and towns, can no longer be taken for granted, but neither do I believe it will it be replaced by the virtual online "forum" on the internet. Physical public spaces still provide the best guarantee of equitable and open and, yes, *unpredictable*, civic engagement.

It's not automatic; protecting public spaces for the public *does* require planning and participation. From places of civic exchange or collective action, urban spaces have in recent decades gradually but persistently seen their transformation into realms tailored for the fundamental neo-liberal enterprise of conspicuous consumption and disposal. Georg Simmel's urban dweller, the *flaneur*, would today find his blasé gaze bombarded with a calculated arsenal of stimuli, lifestyles to be emulated, requiring new products to be purchased and formerly new products rejected. In today's public spaces, it matters little whether these products are available for immediate purchase and consumption in physical retail outlets or they enter our subconscious wish list for convenient retrieval next time we connect to either a virtual portal of ecommerce or the (only slightly less virtual) portal of big box retail. The urban places which this formula produces are vibrant, exciting and bubbling with diversity. At first glance they seem to serve the city's collective needs as urban spaces always have, and in fact, they are often historical spaces transformed. From the radical makeovers of underused infrastructural sites such as Boston's Quincy Market or London's Covent Garden to the subtle but incessant commercialization of European historical landmarks like Rome's Campo de' Fiori, it is evident that while ersatz copies and historically-themed malls may suffice for a market weaned on virtual reality, and the biggest and newest offerings may succeed for short runs, nothing really endures market success like "the real thing," authentic urban spaces co-opted for their aura but emptied of urban functions apart from commerce.

However, beneath the pleasant renderings of civic charm and vitality, the neo-liberal public space of consumption presents several fundamental problems:

Despite a hopeful resurgence in locally produced food and crafts, the vast majority of stuff sold comes from far away, as do the majority of the consumers to whom the stuff is marketed. Both products and public impose a significant transportation burden on the city, importing them from distant locations and removing their byproducts to remote landfills.

Not only do these movements of people and product take a toll on the urban fabric and planetary ecosystem; they also weaken the identity of a place. Rome, with its Byzantine approval process for any change, has held out longer than other European capitals in resisting the onslaught of global branding, and still has no Starbucks[1], but even here, slowly but surely, shops serving urban needs are being transformed into outlets for placeless consumables and services. Ironically, the more visitors flock to a place, drawn by its cultural identity, the stronger the economic pressures to undermine that identity.

Aside from fashion, food and some personal electronics, the vast majority of lifestyle purchases pushed by the neo-liberal system don't actually fit in the public realm where they are advertised but, in fact, work to destroy it, to cancel it out and undermine it: large greenfields real estate developments, automobiles and most of the appliances and furniture with which we are tempted to fill our voids. Italian public spaces are rapidly becoming saturated with cars and other personal appliances that no longer fit in private spaces. And with advertising for more of the same. Amidst this debris wander discontented tourists and few others.

Finally, along with their abandonment by local stakeholders, public places have seen an astounding increase in surveillance and control. The effect is to simultaneously eliminate the anonymity that was for Simmel one of the prime characteristics of the 20th century metropolis, but also to allow the privatization of public space in the name of public order and defense of private property. One thinks of the transformation of the Roman Forum from free public domain to ticketed "heritage site" in the last decades, or the creation of urban *piazze* such as that in front of Zaha Hadid's MAXXI or the Parco della Musica, both born gated and under electronic gaze.

William Mitchell made some incisive observations about the erosion that surveillance enables of the traditional distinctions between public and private space, distinctions that for Nolli were so straightforward. "Security cameras provide interior private spaces with one-way views of public exteriors…while exterior displays occasionally reveal what is going on within a building." Many, including Mitchell himself, expressed trepidation about this "new, pervasive machinery of discipline and control."

Entering Rome at Piazza del Popolo

Senatus Populusque, Roma Capitale and the Common Good

A recent article by journalist and professor of cultural heritage Salvatore Settis blames urban sprawl on "the eclipse of public good and the triumph of private interests."

But we should remember the root of the word *comune* — used in almost all modern Italian cities as it was in the medieval city-states — is defined by *beni comuni* or the common good. Lorenzetti's fresco introduced in Chapter Two depicts the *Comune di Siena* as a collective enterprise, requiring the participation of active citizens working not against one another, except for healthy, short term competition, but together toward common goals. Siena's government in the 13th century was formed by the *popolo* or people, together with a *podestà*, a neutral foreign ruler who kept potential local tyrants in check.

From the middle ages until 2008 the official title of Rome was the *Comune di Roma*, the symbol on its crest the she-wolf and the twins she nursed, Romulus and Remus. This changed with a law that established "Roma Capitale" as a special case, like the District of Columbia, bypassing the limitations of other cities. The term had been used to describe the late 19th century designation of Rome as young Italy's capital, but only now went into effect as an administrative reality. The purported reason was to gain access to financial support reserved for the national government, but the implications are more sinister. Does replacing Comune with Capitale mean bypassing accountability to the people, substituting the "common good" with centralized power? Or worse, is the *capitale* of the economic, not the political variety?

In a similar linguistic paradox, SPQR, engraved by imperial generals on ancient triumphal arches and stamped by city officials on modern iron manhole covers, means that the power of Rome belongs to *Senatus Populusque*, not the government vs. the people but the government *and* the people, both. While it may seem that all power is held (and abused) by overpaid politicians, it is through the work of community groups and participatory design that sustainable change takes places and unhealthy, unsustainable change is thwarted. While the media is drawn to the sensational images of old-economy protests, behind the scenes Rome is teaming with grass-roots initiatives working toward transition into a new urban and regional economy.

Associazioni

There is a long tradition of associations in Italy, formally established or loosely knit groups of people with a mission, strategy and tactical methodology which often ignores or undermines the mainstream preconceptions of political or economic order. While medieval guilds served the interests of a specific group of craftsmen, merchants or professionals, today's movements quite often work toward a more nebulous but far-reaching "public good." Associations are exempt from many of the restrictions, procedures and fees that hamper commercial enterprises in Italy, so many startups begin as associations (as did Scala Reale, my cultural travel venture).

The focus may be on a very specific issue (cyclist rights, urban agriculture, access to water, transit equity, preservation of cultural heritage, environmental justice, etc.) but the strategies are common to many movements. They tend to be creative and use art, theatre, and a strong command of communication to capture attention. A flash mob in 2012 saw 30,000 individuals drawn — by social media — to Piazza del Popolo simultaneously for a Gangnam-style dance exhibition. The potential for engagement is clearly huge. Today's community activists in Rome are often digitally more proficient than mainstream media and administrators, giving them an edge.

Primavera Romana walk in the hinterland within Rome

Walking as an Act of Resistance

A ragtag group of mostly 20-something to 40-something bohemians meet at a peripheral train station and head out for a day in the country. It is actually a day in the city of Rome; most of the 20 plus kilometers we will walk are within the city's administrative boundaries. I had heard about *Primavera Romana* from its organizers, friends in the architectural collaborative called Stalker, founded in the mid 90s and inspired by the Tarkovsky film of the same name. The initiative's aim is to experience the city by walking it, especially those paths less travelled (at least on foot) by normal people.

The leadership is loose-knit, the plan even looser, but after years of experience with such outings the 27 other participants are confident that it will all work out. If there can be said to be leaders of this initiative and these walks, it would be Lorenzo and Giulia. They have mapped out a route to coincide with meetings with local stakeholders, particularly in the area of Castel di Guido where one of two city-owned working farms still persists. This is our first destination and Lorenzo leads the way.

Castel di Guido is comprised of several thousand hectares of farmland surrounding a *borgata agricola*, a farming village which still boasts a public school, a day-care center, a public health clinic, a community center, a museum of rural culture and more. Founded by the church-run Santo Spirito hospital to provide food for patients, it became Italian after the unification of Italy 150 years ago and is today faced with the threat of development. Instead of producing revenue for the city the property is actually costing Rome money to maintain, an absurdity which can only be blamed on ineffective management and confused priorities which see in land the promise of economic profit before food. The farm staff has been reduced to a fraction of what it was even 50 years ago but they still produce and sell the results in Rome at the weekend farmers market in Testaccio. We lunch on lentils and soup, local salamis and cheeses and good red wine (a deal at 6 euro per person contribution). We hear from some of the current and former farm workers who are keeping alive the oral history of the farm. We view a video produced by the local associations with interviews and images of the women from the farm.

After lunch the walk takes a different course, in single file along roads made for cars, not people, zigzagging around fenced properties, revising plans on the fly as the logistics of limited Sunday train schedules and the slow speed of trekking required. At one point we find ourselves at a truck stop, probably the only pedestrians ever to have ventured there. Night falls and we are still pretty far from the train station where we were to have continued the itinerary (but are now merely hoping to find a lift back to "Rome"). And what's more, it is getting cold. I am glad my phone's GPS is still working, and the bike light I keep on my backpack provides a small safety beacon as cars zip past us in the dark.

Like many other "alternative" events in which I've participated, what might, according to conventional standards, seem a failure is actually celebrated. The simple fact of occupying, on foot and in company, routes not intended for people shakes up the system and calls into question what we accept as "normal." I think I've finally found a group of urban observers even crazier than me.

Michel de Certeau, in *The Practice of Everyday Life*, talks of walking in the city "as a space of enunciation," and the act of walking in the city has become increasingly political act. Groups (or, better, phenomena) like *Stalker* or *Primavera Romana* are now common vehicles for urban discourse. Walking has taken off as a form of civic engagement. In addition to *Primavera Romana*, we see "urban trekking" programs which started in Siena, linked to longer pilgrimages along the Via Francigena. *Urban Experience* organizes "walk shows" and my own *Ecological Itineraries* project orchestrates participatory architectural walks through neighborhoods and the urban fringes. I have been walking the city consciously since my arrival, not like Richard Long's conceptual artworks, "Line Made by Walking," but as a way of unveiling and explaining the city. I like to think that Scala Reale was at the forefront of this movement, but the tradition of walking to experience place goes back to the beginning of the human race.

Ciclofficini and other *Centri Sociali*

Ivan Illich said that change should take place at the speed of the bicycle, and the role of the cycling movement in urban transformation seems to confirm this. Cycling is not just about transportation or recreation; a strong part of the movement relates to the communities of people that form around the construction and repair of vehicles themselves. Rome has a dozen *ciclofficini* (in English often called bike kitchens) which become de-facto centers for grassroots ferment. One of the most central, *Ciclonauti* in the Monti neighborhood in view of the Forum of Augustus, places a key role in the movement to promote cycling rights. Organized as an association, you can join and use the workshop and tools to build or repair your own bike. When an association I direct organized a clean-up of the Tiber river banks recently and were looking for a cargo bike to haul trash, *Ciclonauti* were happy to lend us a bike trailer.

Other *ciclofficini* share space with larger *centri sociali*, alternative social centers which in Italy are often at the center of political (almost always left-wing) agitation and advocacy. From the central Rialto Sant'Ambrogio near the former Jewish ghetto, to the outlying Forte Prenestino, these centers occupy unused buildings, often as squatters without legal rights but with clear objectives and internal rules and regulations to prevent vandalism. As we saw in the chapter on Waste, Rome has a long tradition of adaptive reuse of which the occupation of abandoned buildings by squatters is just one manifestation.

Forte Prenestino is one of the city's dozen or so military forts, built as part of a costly and suspect public works project during the establishment of the first "Roma Capitale" but never used by a single soldier since Rome has never since been attacked. Standing empty in the late 70s, and earmarked officially for public services which never materialized, it was occupied by local youth in 1986 and has since hosted concerts, courses and a wide range of cultural events. Down the street, closer to Rome, former synthetic silk factories were occupied in the 1990s as a social center called the ex-Snia. Here the community runs a *ciclofficina*, an edible garden, and many other activities[2]. Street art abounds in the buildings and surrounding neighborhood, but the most astounding presence is the artificial lake discovered recently in the abandoned industrial wilderness, and "liberated" for use by the community.

Next door to the Ex-Snia squat, an imposing structure of steel and glass with photovoltaic panels incorporated into its roof stands empty most of the time. Called the Parco delle Energie, this was a city sponsored project completed in early 2000s with the aim of revitalizing an underutilized public park. It is hard to ignore the contrast between this expensive and abandoned top-down project with the vibrant (illegal) activities next door at the *Centro Sociale*.

Blogging Statues

In ancient Rome, in order to get the word out about an alternative project, or to voice concerns about top-down policies, you could climb the steps to the Rostrum in the Roman Forum and orate to anyone interested in listening. Up until a few years ago, despite advances in the free press, the only direct way to communicate your views was to call upon the "talking statues." Situated around the center, these are sculpted figures, fountains, busts, or fragments of ancient monuments that provided convenient reference points for illicit expression; at night people would secretively hang notes around the statues or post them on the walls nearby, to be read the following morning before being removed by the authorities.

Thanks to the internet, the talking statues are no longer needed (although the tradition does persist at Pasquino, off Piazza Navona, and occasionally at the *Babuino* on the *Via* of the same name). Today anyone can blog and tweet and otherwise blast their ideas and observations to anyone willing to listen. Apart from the many food and travel sites, one of the most successful phenomena in the Roman blogosphere, as measured in hits and comments, has been the plethora of blogs denouncing urban blight. The list is long, including several I created personally to voice my observations (and vent my frustrations), but the prize for brutal candor and willingness to call a spade a spade goes to *Roma Fa Schifo*. One of a number of related blogs launched by journalist Massimiliano Tonelli (whose day jobs have him reporting on food and art), RFS has gained a key place in the changing landscape of city journalism. Newspapers in Rome have always been the sounding boards for political parties, left or right, but RFS is blatantly free from such simplifications and earns venomous attacks from both extremes. Posts might expose the mafia of illegal billboards, food trucks and parking attendants or call upon police to arrest Rom children begging and stealing on the metro. Knee-jerk reactions from the liberal media calling for sympathetic turning of blind eyes for minor offenses are met with disdain by RFS, often citing the broken window syndrome whereby a small violation left unpunished results quickly in total anarchy as institutions are perceived as impotent. Apart from the content, mostly composed of simple observations and opinions with little attempt at journalistic rigor, the sheer number of hits and comments on RFS is impressive and signals a paradigm shift. The fatalism for which Romans are famous ("che sara' sara', whatever will be, will be") is starting to give way to a mass exasperation with the declining state of the city. Citizens are starting to shout *"basta"* — enough is enough.

And they are doing more than complaining. Apps like WeDU and *IoSegnalo* enable citizens to document and denounce violations of urban decorum and post them to a site monitored by city authorities. Most impressively, Rome's new Police Commissioner, Raffaele Clemente encourages citizens to tweet their observations to a dedicated twitter handle @PLRomaCapitale; almost without exception the police act quickly on these tweets and report on the results (towed cars, etc.).

The participation goes beyond the digital to act on location in the physical world. Volunteers, both Italian and foreign born, join organizations like Retake, started by a group of American expats and Romans as a response to frustration with trash and graffiti, to go out and clean neighborhoods. The trend is growing and attracting the attention of the administration.

Navigating Caput Mundi

How does Rome's visibility as a seat of global culture lend support to local movements for change? One of my working assumptions, along with "small is the new big" is that "everything is local somewhere."

In the previous chapter I introduced the walking tours I design as a rich means of transportation; here we return to them in the context of global and local identity and community participation.

The design of the itineraries, like a good architectural project, grows from attention to the specifics of site, leveraging what is already there, whether fixed artifacts or fleeting phenomena. Furthermore, as seminars, the questions and contributions of participants affects the itinerary. A discussion of Baroque theatricality might, for example, spur a sudden detour to the Trevi Fountain. Even local input, in the form of a religious procession, a political demonstration or simply advice from a local shop-keeper, can divert the route unexpectedly. Just as science has come to accept that there are no non-intrusive investigations, these walking tours affirm that interacting with cities is the only choice. In fact, rather than aiming for low-impact, they seek to have a positive impact on the city, both financial — by directing the spending power of the participants to local, civic-minded recipients — and social, by promoting cultural interaction.

While the case of Scala Reale is interesting for the conscious design and organization of fine-tuned yet flexible itineraries, it is really just an extreme case of how we all take action in cities. To varying degrees, we are all informed and empowered navigators. We plan our routes based on criteria ranging from speed to scenic value. We are ready to detour as conditions require, even to tap into local knowledge for advice (do you know a good restaurant?) and feedback (is the Colosseum that way?). We read signs, whether explicit or subliminal, and make our moves accordingly.

Today our tools are more sophisticated than ever and their advancement has been so rapid as to constitute a revolution, not a mere improvement. Last week while planning a trip to Paris using Google Streetview I literally roamed the streets of the Marais on my computer looking for a hotel, and when I found something that looked promising (because I liked the feel of the street, the style of the facade, the sign above the door) I popped open another tab to browse photos of rooms, reviews by recent guests, prices and availability for my stay. Before long other senses, at least the sounds of the city, will be integrated into the experience and our tools will become richer still.

How ironic, then, that we are witnessing a parallel process of isolation from the diversity of the city: tourists on tour buses,

Romans closed in air-conditioned cars, immigrants on public transit with surprisingly little overlap. Ironic but not coincidental; as Hannah Arendt said, "action is never possible in isolation" and there are economic and political powers whose interests would be threatened by any popular action except, of course, acquisition and consumption. Will our tools for navigation end up providing a virtual substitute for real navigation in the real metropolis? Will a corporate-induced fear of the public realm drive people to seek the fastest and safest routes to final destinations where they can at last immerse themselves in hyper-realistic, high-definition simulations of urban scenarios? Such dystopian imagery, while sparking a certain macabre fascination, doesn't have to become our urban reality. Instead of fearing the perceived chaos of urban experience as a threat and seeking to tame it with technology or barricade ourselves from it with wealth, we should celebrate it and bask in its aura.

If there is one thing that both genetic research and Web 2.0 have shown us it is that the best outcome emerges when complexity and diversity are nurtured, when a complex fabric, rich with attractions and restraints, is populated by concerned stakeholders and traversed by informed navigators. Down from the double-decker buses, out from the motorcade, into the streets, cities like Rome are ready for true, hands-on, global community action.

Notes

1. At printing time in March 2016 Starbucks has announced it will open in Milan.

2. Architect Fritz Haeg, the author of the book Edible Gardens, donated

to the Ex-Snia the experimental garden that he had developed in fruit crates as a fellow at the American Academy in 2010.

CHAPTER 8.

CONCLUSIONS: EMERGENCY, OPPORTUNITY AND TRANSITION

These seven themes, conceived as useful organizational devices, nevertheless refuse to remain separate; like Rome itself, they overlap and contaminate one another. The Theatre of Marcellus, a great example of the adaptive reuse of urban fabric to eliminate waste, can also be seen in the context of green space, water management, and even transportation (given the bus terminus on the site of the former stage). The flow of water through the city is dictated by the urban fabric and by green spaces, but Rome's river also has presented opportunities for mobility, at least when it was still navigable. Mobility, along with buildings, is a major consumer of energy, but central Rome's dense urban fabric, and the presence of productive agricultural land within city limits, makes "proximity power" our best energy strategy. The elimination of waste, in turn, frees up (and provides nutrients for) green space. And with all of these issues, for change to take place in a lasting manner, will require community participation.

Planting the seeds of change requires a combination of scientific method and creative thinking, which has always been a good architect's modus operandi. It also depends on transparency, inter-disciplinary collaboration, communication and participation, traits for which architects of late have been less known. If anything ties together the seven themes addressed in this book, it is the fact that they have all been revolutionized, for better or for worse, in the last fifty years.

The Last Half Century

The year I was born, 1961, Buckminster Fuller launched the World Game project, whose goal was a global simulation to make the world work for 100% of humanity in the shortest period of time. That same year the Berlin Wall went up, the first genetic Poly-U experiments were performed, and the first human being went into space. It was the year the Peace Corps and the World Wildlife Fund and the World Food Program were founded, the year of the Bay of Pigs. The first quasar was discovered by Allan Sandage at Mt Palomar, California. Mumford published *The City in History* and Jane Jacobs wrote *Life and Death of the Great American City*. JFK was sworn in as President (and future-President Barack Obama was born.) The Beatles performed for the first time that year. Eight days before I was born Ernest Hemingway shot himself in the head in Ketchum, Idaho.

In Italy that year, the nation celebrated its centennial, and began the period of prosperity that would be termed the *miracolo italiano*. The design magazine *Abitare* first hit the newsstands. Harvard University inherited the Villa I Tatti outside Florence. Pasolini's *Accatone* and Federico Fellini's *La Dolce Vita* were both in cinemas, showing the two extremes of Roman society. Recently re-watching Michelangelo Antonio's *L'Eclisse*, a beautiful film depicting a day in the modern city of Rome, from the E.U.R. (Esposizione Universale di Roma) quarter to Piazza di Pietra, I saw the dateline on the newspaper Monica Vitti was reading and realized the entire film was set on the day I was born.

Since that day the population of the planet has doubled and Buckminster Fuller's goals of making the planet work are farther than ever from becoming a reality. In fact, we have seen the divide between rich and poor grow greater and greater, with the top one percent now earning 20 of all income and owning 35 percent of the world's wealth.

When I was six I went to Expo '67 in Montreal and saw two works of architecture which would remain with me and influence my thinking: Bucky Fuller's Geodesic Dome and Moshe Safdie's Habitat. Safdie's romantic pseudo-village thrilled me with its forms, like things I was making with legos, but big. I had never seen a medieval hill town but Habitat excited in me the same sense of fascination with the process of accretion through which cities grow (although in hindsight it was really just a massive single development, not unlike the real estate ventures, shopping malls, etc. that Safdie would create in later years).

The Expo Dome left a bigger impression and I became quite interested in Fuller's ideas, especially the simple triangular-based, geodesic geometries which provided the maximum spatial enclosure using the minimum material and energy expenditures. Between the simplicity of Fuller's dome (too simple to adapt smoothly to local conditions, to nest with neighboring structures or to contain our boxy stuff) and Safdie's contrived vernacular I started to get the passion for cities that would bring me to Rome[1].

A few years after our trip to Montreal my parents were having tea on our porch in the Boston suburbs and an elderly man walked across the lawn and introduced himself as Bucky Fuller. He told them how, as a child, walking past the house on his way to Milton Academy, he would occasionally pick flowers in our yard. At the time I was holed up in my attic world, most likely assembling geodesic domes out of toothpicks, and they didn't bother calling me. But I did meet Fuller years later at a long and crazy lecture at Boston's Wang Center, and mourned when he passed away the year I finished college. I often quote his observations on the trimtab ("call me trimtab" is all it says on his tomb):

> "Something hit me very hard once, thinking about what one little man could do. Think of the Queen Mary—the whole ship goes by and then comes the rudder. And there's a tiny thing at the edge of the rudder called a trim tab.
>
> It's a miniature rudder. Just moving the little trim tab builds a low pressure that pulls the rudder around. Takes almost no effort at all. So I said that the little individual can be a trim tab. Society thinks it's going right by you, that it's left you altogether. But if you're doing dynamic things mentally, the fact is that you can just put your foot out like that and the whole big ship of state is going to go."

Like all complex systems, cities evolve in non-linear ways.

Unforeseen changes can be caused by seemingly small events, the proverbial final straw. Donella Meadows, who wrote *Limits to Growth* in Rome the same year as Fuller's statement above, reminds us that you can usually modify an element and the system will endure but changing a rule or purpose can lead to huge and sometimes crazy results.

Rome has the advantage of inertia; its historic fabric has ensured resilience and resistance to change. Ironically its slow reaction time has allowed it to leapfrog over the mistakes made by more efficient civilizations, such as the replacement of energy efficient old buildings with new and stylish but wasteful ones when petroleum was cheap. Efficiency, as a goal, has lost is allure, and destructive efficiency is the bane of our time. Unfortunately, as William McDonough and Michael Braungart note, "Efficient destruction is harder to detect and thus harder to stop." Fortunately, efficiency has never had much currency in Rome. Resiliency, recycling, richness, beauty, yes, but not efficiency. This, however, doesn't mean we should be satisfied with the way things are. As architect Thom Mayne said in a 2007 TED talk "to be conservative is the riskiest approach today."

Human impact on the planet has increased at an exponential pace; we consume more land, forests, waters, fossil-fuels, and materials and we waste an increasing percentage of what we claim to consume. Yet humans throughout history have demonstrated a distinct capacity to reason and create, "to imbue matter with spirit" to paraphrase the words of Paolo Soleri. Such a capacity should counter, not fuel, our consumptive tendencies. What do we call the injection of knowledge and spirit into material to transform it into something with greater enduring value? The key prerequisite or skills might be creativity and scientific reasoning, but put them together and the phenomenon goes by the simple word "design." The same raw travertine mighty be transformed into a fountain like the Trevi and inform and delight urban dwellers for eternity or it might be used to furnish the boardroom of a corporation that goes bankrupt before its completion and fall to the wrecking ball never having been used. Smart design can ensure that the stone is used and enjoyed by many without necessitating its division. Life forms continue to evolve toward a more orderly state, thus resisting the natural tendency toward entropy. Teillhard de Chardin frames this in spiritual terms as evolution "towards increasing consciousness" but it can also be seen in scientific terms as greater order through greater complexity.

The public art of Baroque Rome is a good example of this anti-entropic tendency. Bernini and green design? Yes, in the sense that a work like the Fountain of the Four Rivers lifts its simple blocks of Travertine and marble from mute, expendable materials to narrative through design. Most of what we rely on today to achieve happiness comes at an environmental price, but not stories. So when a work of architecture or public art communicates through narrative, it spreads enjoyment at no cost to the planet. And the longer it is in use, especially if it changes its use over time, the richer and more enjoyable its stories, and the longer the period over which its material costs are amortized.

Borromini's dome of Sant'Ivo alla Sapienza, 1660

Often the aims of sustainability and those of cultural heritage seem to clash, environmental advocates drawn into battle against historic preservationists over energy efficient windows or photovoltaic panels that, in the eyes of some people, mar older buildings. But the positive effects of prolonging the life of existing buildings are usually superior to the drawbacks of letting them fall into disuse by banning all modifications. It may not make sense to install solar panels on tile roofs, but on the other hand, the energy footprint of the older building is already less than much of what was built in the last 50 years.

In Rome, human culture and the natural environment find a common ground in the age old experience of urban living. The world's most resilient city, Rome has always bounced back from the stresses and strains of history. It has never stopped evolving, and never finished the task of weaving a complex web of interlocking urban systems. Today the threats and the potential are greater than ever. The challenge of Rome, the challenge that keeps me and so many others in Rome, despite all the obstacles, is to steer it back onto a sustainable course without jettisoning its rich culture.

Notes

1. For more on the reasons I stay in Rome see
   https://sustainablerome.wordpress.com/2011/05/10/if-you-don't-like-it-here/

AFTERWARD

Envisioning Rome

You are on a train from Berlin, heading into Rome, *Anno 2030,* decades after your last trip there. The uncontaminated country- side is punctuated by hilltop villages and farms which continue well within the city limits. A green belt has been reinstated and is richly cultivated, with 90 percent of Rome's food coming from local producers.

Many of the more wasteful constructions of the post-war years have been dismantled, their materials contributing to the active material banks for use retrofitting the consolidated city, pro- viding work for a stable population. Through a combination of energy efficient retrofitting, lifestyle improvements and conver- sion of rooftops to power plants, the city has become carbon neutral. Solar pergolas provide shade and shelter in public spaces and on roof terraces, producing energy for civic needs.

The historical center has long since become a pedestrian zone, eliminating the dangers and annoyances of motor vehicles. Chil- dren play in the streets, elderly stop to chat without the noise and intimidation of cars. In fact, with the auto industry no longer dominating space needs, real estate costs have dropped and young entrepreneurs have started up ventures in transition technologies throughout the city. In place of former auto showrooms there are now bakeries, publishing houses and nursery schools. Gas stations and car dealerships have been removed, leaving more room for people. Private vehicle still exist, of course, but they are fast, safe, clean and beautiful... and kept in storage at convenient locations on the edge of town, like skis in the attic, waiting to be used when appropriate, such as trips to the countryside or occasional moving jobs.

But Rome really hasn't changed. The midday sun casts sharp shadows onto the tuff blocks of the Servian Walls, the fountains are again bubbling with fresh water from natural springs, and the *piazza* is bustling with people. Vintage clothes and architectural salvage materials are being sold in former parking lots. The smell of pizza and roast meats wafts across the square where tables are set up and people sit drinking and dining in the shade of pine trees. As you board the hydrogen powered tram which will shuttle you past the Baths of Diocletian and down Via Nazionale to your Air BnB overlooking the world's largest archaeological site, the Roman Forum, you watch and overhear a group of Roman youth gesticulating passionately. "What do you expect, this is Rome, things will never change!"

BIBLIOGRAPHY

Ackerman, James. "Gathering the Given: Michelangelo's Redesign of the Campidoglio". in *Harvard Design Magazine* Fall 2005/Winter 2006.

Aicher, Peter. *Guide to the Aqueducts of Ancient Rome*, Mundelein, Illinois: Bolchazy-Carducci Publishers. 1995.

Alexander, Christopher. *A Pattern Language*. Oxford: Oxford University Press. 1977.

Alexander, Christopher. *Notes on the Synthesis of Form*. Cambridge, MA: Harvard University Press. 1964.

Allen Stan, "Field Conditions" in *Points and Lines: Diagrams and Projects for the City*. New York, N.Y.: Princeton Architectural Press. 1999.

Architecture for Humanity, ed. *Design Like You Give a Damn*. New York: Metropolis Books. 2006.

Ashby, Thomas. *The Aqueducts of Ancient Rome*. Oxford: Oxford University Press, 1935.

Bacon, Edmund N. *Design of Cities*. New York: Penguin Books. 1967. (reprint 1978).

Banfield, Edward C. *The Moral Basis of a Backward Society.* New York: Simon and Schuster, The Free Press, 1958.

Banham Reyner, *Theory and Design in the First Machine Age.* New York: Princeton Architectural Press. 1960.

Banham, Reyner. *The Architecture of the Well-tempered Environment.* Chicago: University of Chicago Press. 1969.

Bateson, Gregory. *Mind and Nature.* New York: E.P. Dutton. 1979.

Benedikt, Michael, *For an Architecture of Reality.* New York, Lumen Books 1987.

Benjamin, Walter. *Art in the Age of Mechanical Reproduction.* Cambridge: Belknap Press. 2008.

Berger, Alan. "Urban Land is a Natural Thing to Waste" in *Harvard Design Magazine.* Fall 2005/Winter 2006. Cambridge, MA : MIT Press. 2006.

Berger, Alan. *Drosscape.* Princeton, NJ: Princeton Architectural Press. 2006.

Betsky, Aaron, ed. *Uneternal City: Urbanism Beyond Rome.* Catalogue of exhibit of 2008 Biennale di Architettura.

Boatwright, M., D. Gargola, and R. Talbert. *From Village to Empire: The Romans and Their History.* New York: Oxford University Press. 2004.

Brand, Stewart. *How Buildings Learn.* New York: Viking. 1994.

Brandi, Cesare. *Theory of Restoration.* Firenze; Nardini. 2005. (orig. 1977)

Brown, Lester. *Plan B 3.0: Mobilizing to Save Civilization.* New York: W.W. Norton & Co. 2008.

Buchanan, Peter. *Ten Shades Of Green.* New York: Architectural League of New York. 2005.

Calthorpe, Peter. *The Next American Metropolis: Ecology, Community, and the American Dream.* New York, Princeton University Press 1993.

Calthorpe, Peter. *The Regional City: New Urbanism and the End of Sprawl.* Washington,DC, Island Press, 2000.

Calvino, Italo. *Invisible Cities.* translated by William Weaver. New York: Harcourt Brace. 1974.

Carson, Rachel. *Silent Spring.* Boston: Houghton Mifflin. 1962.

Carver, Norman F. *Italian Hilltowns.* Kalamazoo, MI: Documan Press. 1979.

Casciato, Maristella. "Rome Cannot Bear the Present" in *Harvard Design Magazine,* Summer 1999.

Christopher Hibbert. *Rome: the Biography of a City.* London: Penguin. 1985.

CIAM "Charter of Athens: tenets" (1933) in Conrads, Ulrich, ed. *Programs and Manifestoes on 20th-Century Architecture.* Cambridge, MA: MIT Press. 1975

Claridge, Amanda. *Rome: An Oxford Archaeological Guide.* New York: Oxford. 1998

Coldstream, Nicola. *Art and Architecture in Italy, 1250-1400.* New Haven: Yale University Press Pelican History of Art. 1993.

Colquhoun A., "Typology and Design Method", in *Arena, Vol. 83*, June 1976.

Colquhoun, Alan. *Modern Architecture*. London: Oxford Paperbacks. 2002

Commoner, Barry. *Making Peace with the Planet*. New York: Pantheon Books. 1990.

Conant, Kenneth John. *Carolingian and Romanesque Architecture 800-1200*. New Haven: Yale University Press Pelican History of Art. 1992.

Constant "New Babylon" (1960) in Conrads, Ulrich, ed. *Programs and Manifestoes on 20th-Century Architecture*. Cambridge, MA: MIT Press. 1975

Corrado Augias. *The Secrets of Rome*. New York, Rizzoli, 2007.

Crawford, Margaret, "Blurring the Boundaries" in: Chase, Crawford, Kaliski (eds), *Everyday Urbanism*. The Monacelli Press: New York. 1999.

D'Ambra, E., ed.. *Roman Art in Context: An Anthology*. Englewood Cliffs, NJ:

Denise Scott Brown, "The art in waste." talk given to Basurama, Madrid. c.2001

Diamond, Jared. *Collapse: How Societies Choose to Fail or Succeed*. New York: Viking. 2005.

Doxiadis, C. A. *Ecology and Ekistics*. Boulder, CO: Westview Press. 1977.

Duany, Andres, Elizabeth Plater-Zyberk adn Jeff Speck, *Suburban*

Nation: The Rise of Sprawl and the Decline of the American Dream.
New York: North Point Press. 2000.

Eck, Caroline van. *Organicism in Nineteenth-Century Architecture: An Inquiry into its Theoretical and Philosophical Background.* Amsterdam: Architectura & Natura Press. 1994.

Edwards, C. 1996. *Writing Rome: Textual Approaches to the City.* Cambridge: Cambridge University Press.

Eigen, Edward. "The Housing of Entropy: Schrödinger's Code-Script." in *Perspecta 35* (2004).

Favro, Diane, ed. *Streets: Critical Perspective on Public Space.* Berkeley: University of California Press, 1996

Favro, Diane. *The Urban Image of Augustan Rome.* Cambridge: Cambridge University Press. 1998.

Fitch, James Marston. *American Building 2: The Environmental Forces that Shape It.* 1971.

Flavin, Christopher and Nicholas Lenssen. *Beyond the Petroleum Age: Designing the Solar Economy.* Worldwatch Paper 100. Washington DC: Worldwatch Institute. 1990.

Foucault, Michel, "Of Other Spaces" in *Diacritics 16,* 1986 (now in public domain).

Frampton, Kenneth; 1998. "Towards a critical regionalism: six points for an Architecture of Resistance" in Foster, Hal ed. *The Anti-Aesthetic: essays on postmodern culture.* The New Press: New York; 17-34.

Frampton, Kenneth. *Modern Architecture: A Critical History.* London: Thames & Hudson Ltd;. 1992.

Frampton, Kenneth. *Studies in Tectonic Culture.* 1995.

Fuller, R. Buckminster "The Architect as World Planner" (1961) in Conrads, Ulrich, ed. *Programs and Manifestoes on 20th-Century Architecture.* Cambridge, MA: MIT Press. 1975

Fuller, R. Buckminster. *Critical Path.* New York: St. Martin's Press. 1981.

Fuller, R. Buckminster. *Earth, Inc.* Garden City, NY: Anchor Press. 1973.

Fuller, R. Buckminster. *Utopia or Oblivion: The Prospects for Humanity.* 1969.

Galison, Peter and Caroline Jones. "Factory, Laboratory, Studio." in *The Architecture of Science.* 1999.

Gandelsonas, M., "The Identity of the American City," "The City as the Object of Architecture," "Drawing The American City," in *X-Urbanism: Architecture and the American City.* New York, N.Y.: Princeton Architectural Press, 1999.

Garreau, Joel. *Edge City: Life on the New Frontier.* New York: Double Day 1991.

Giedion, Seigfried. *Space, Time, and Architecture: The Growth of a New Tradition.* 1941 (esp. on Sixtus V and the Planning of Baroque Rome). Cambridge, MA: Harvard University Press. 2009.

Goethe, Joann Wolfgang Von. *Italian Journeys.* translated by W.H.Auden and Elizabeth Mayer. San Francisco: North Point. 1982.

Gonzalo, Roberto and Karl J. Habermann, *Energy Efficient Architecture.* Birkhäuser. Basel Switzerland. 2006.

Gore, Al. *An Inconvenient Truth: The Planetary Emergency of Global Warming and What We Can Do About It.* Emmaus, PA: Rodale. 2006.

Gore, Al. *Earth in the Balance.* New York: Houghton Mifflin. 1992.

Gottman, Jean. *Megalopolis.* Cambridge, MA: MIT Press. 1961.

Hartmann, Thomas. *The Last Hours of Ancient Sunlight.* New York: Three Rivers Press. 2004.

Heiken, Grant, et. al. *The Seven Hills of Rome: a Geological Tour of the Eternal City.* Princeton: Princeton University Press. 2005

Heschong, Lisa. *Thermal Delights in Architecture.* Cambridge, MA: MIT Press. 1970.

Hewitt, Mark and Susannah Hagan. *City Fights. Debates on Urban Sustainability.* London: James and James. 2001.

Heydenreich , Ludwig H. *Architecture in Italy, 1400-1500.* New Haven: Yale University Press Pelican History of Art.;

Hitchcock, Henry-Russell. *Architecture. Nineteenth and Twentieth Centuries.* New Haven, CT: The Yale University Press. 1992.

Hopkins, John, "The Cloaca Maxima" in *Waters of Rome, n. 4*, March 2007

Hough, Michael. 1984. *City Form and Natural Process.* New York: Van Nostrand Reinbold. 1984.

Howard, Deborah. *The Architectural History of Venice* (Revised and enlarged edition) New Haven: Yale University Press Pelican History of Art. 2004.

Howard, Ebenezer. *Garden Cities of Tomorrow.* 1898. Reprinted by Cambridge, MA: MIT Press. 1965.

Huyssen, Andreas. *Present Pasts: Urban Palimpsests and the Politics of Memory.* Stanford, CA: Stanford University Press. 2003.

Illich, Ivan. "Energy and Equity" in Stephen Lyons, ed. *Sun.* New York: Friends of the Earth. 1974.

Ingersoll, Richard. "A Post-Apocalyptic View of Design" in *Harvard Design Magazine.* Spring Summer 2003.

Jackson, John B. *Discovering the Vernacular Landscape.* New Haven: Yale University Press. 1984.

Jackson, Wes. *New Roots for Agriculture.* Lincoln: University of Nebraska Press. 1980.

Jacobs, Allan, "Seeing Change" in Wheeler, Stephen M. and Timothy Beatley, ed. *The Sustainable Urban Development Reader.* London and New York: Routledge. 2004.

Jacobs, Jane. *Life and Death of the Great American City.* Cambridge, MA: M.I.T. Press, 1961.

Johnson, Steven. *The Connected Lives of Ants, Brains, Cities and Software.* London: Penguin Books. 2002.

Jon Michael Schwarting "The Lessons of Rome" in *Harvard Architecture Review, vol. 2.* Cambridge, MA : MIT Press. 1981.

Jones, Kay Bea "Rome's Uncertain Tiberscape: Tevereterno and the Urban Commons" in Rinne, K. ed. *The Waters of Rome* N. 6. Feb 2009.

Jones, Mark Wilson. *Principles of Roman Architecture.* New Haven, CT: Yale University Press. 2003.

Kato, Akinori, "The Plaza in the Italian Culture", *Process Architecture No. 16: Plazas of Southern Europe*. Tokyo: Process Architecture Publishing, 1980. pp. 5-24.

Kelbaugh, Doug. *Repairing the American metropolis: Common place revisited*. Washington: University of Washington Press. 2002.

Kidder Smith, G. E. *Italy Builds: Its Modern Architecture and Native Inheritance*. New York: Reinhold Publishing Corporation. 1954

King, Ross. *Emancipating Space: Geography, Architecture and Urban Design*. New York: Guilford Press. 1996.

Kirk, Terry. *The Architecture of Modern Italy*. Princeton, NJ: Princeton Architectural Press. 2005.

Kolbert, Elizabeth. *Field Notes from a Catastrophe*. London. Bloomsbury 2006.

Koolhaas R., *S, M, L, XL*. New York: Monacelli Press, 1995.

Koolhaas, Rem, Stefano Boeri and Sanford Kwinter. *Mutations. Harvard Project on the City*. Bordeaux: ACTAR, arch en reve centre d'architecture. 2001. esp. p. 10 "How to Build a City: Roman Operating System". and p. 356 "Notes for an research program" by Stefano Boeri.

Kostof, Spiro, "His Majesty the Pick: The Aesthetics of Demolitionj" in *Streets: Critical Perspectives on Public Space*. Z. Celik et. al. (eds.). Berkeley: University of California Press, 1994.

Kostof, Spiro. *The City Assembled: The Elements of Urban Form Through History*. London: Thames & Hudson Ltd;. 1992.

Kostof, Spiro. *The City Shaped: Urban Patterns and Meaning Through History*. London: Bulfinch;. 1991.

Krautheimer, Richard. *Early Christian and Byzantine Architecture.* New Haven: Yale University Press Pelican History of Art. 1992.

Krautheimer, Richard. *Rome, Profile of a City 312-1308.* Princeton, NJ: Princeton University Press. 2000.

Kunstler, James Howard. *The Geography of Nowhere: The Rise and Decline of America's Man-Made Landscape.* New York: Simon and Schuster. 1994.

Kwinter, Sanford. *Architectures of Time: Toward a Theory of the Event in Modernist Culture.* Cambridge: MIT Press. 2001.

Le Corbusier, *Journey to the East.* Cambridge, MA: MIT Press, 2007.

Le Corbusier. *Towards and Architecture* (originally pub. as Vers une Architecture. 1925.) New York: Praeger. 1960.

Leopold, Aldo. *A Sand County Almanac.* Oxford: Oxford University Press. 1949.

Lerup, Lars. *After the City.* Cambridge, MA: MIT Press. 2001.

Lotz, Wolfgang. *Architecture in Italy, 1500-1600.* New Haven: Yale University Press Pelican History of Art. 1995

Lovelock, James. *The Ages of Gaia: A Biography of our Living Earth.* New York: W.W.Norton and Company. 1988.

Lovins, Amory. *Soft Energy Paths: Toward a Durable Peace.* Cambridge, MA: Ballinger Publishing. 1977.

Lyle, John Tillman. *Regenerative Design for Sustainable Development.* John Wiley and Sons, Inc. 1994. esp. "Waste as a Resource"

Lynch, Kevin. "The Waste of Place" in *Places: Vol. 6*: No. 2. 1990.

Lynch, Kevin. *The Image of the City.* Cambridge, MA: MIT Press. 1960.

Marks, Robert. *The Dymaxion World of Buckminster Fuller.* 1960.

Marx, Leo. *The Machine in the Garden: Technology and the Pastoral Ideal in America.* Oxford: Oxford University Press. 1964.

Mau, Bruce. *Massive Change.* New York: Phaedon. 2004.

McDonough, William and Michael Braungart. *Cradle to Cradle: Remaking the Way We Make Things.* New York: North Point Press, 2002.

McHarg, Ian. *Design with Nature.* 1969. New York: John Wiley and Sons. 1992 reprint

Meadows, Donella et. al. *The Limits to Growth* (Abstract). Club of Rome. 1972. with Addendum "30 year update".

Metzger Habel, Dorothy. *The Urban Development of Rome in the Age of Alexander VII.* London: Cambridge University Press. 2002.

Mitchell, William J. *Me++ The Cyborg Self and the Networked City.* MIT Press, 2004.

Morton, Henry Canova Vollam. *The Fountains of Rome.* New York: Macmillan, 1966.

Mumford, Lewis. "The Human Prospect" in *Interpretations and Forecasts 1922-1972.* New York: Harcourt, Brace and World. 1979.

Mumford, Lewis. *The City in History.* New York: Harcourt, Brace and World. 1961.

Mumford, Lewis. *The Highway and the City.* New York: Mentor Books. 1963.

Murray, Peter. *The Architecture of the Italian Renaissance.* London: Thames and Hudson, 1986.

Nesbitt, Kate, ed. *Theorizing a New Agenda for Architecture. An Anthology of Architectural Theory 1965-1995.* Princeton, NJ: Princeton Architectural Press. 1996.

Norberg-Sculz, Christian. *Genius Loci: Towards a Phenomenology of Architecture.* New York: Rizzoli. 1991.

Olgyay, Victor. *Design with Climate.* Princeton , NJ: Princeton University Press. 1963.

Orr, David. "Ecological Literacy: Education for the 21st Century". *Holistic Education Review,* Fall 1987.

Orr, David. *Design on the Edge: The Making of a High Performance Building.* Cambridge, MA: MIT Press. 2006.

Painter, Borden. *Mussolini's Rome: The Fascist Transformation of the Eternal City.* London: Palgrave Macmillan. 2005.

Pawley, Martin. *Future Systems: The Story of Tomorrow.* London: Phaidon Press Ltd. 1993.

Pérez-Gómez, Alberto. *Architecture and the Crisis of Modern Science.* Cambridge: MIT Press. 1983.

Picon, Antoine. "Architecture, Science, Technology, and the Virtual." in *Architecture and the Sciences.* New York: Princeton Architectural Press. 2003.

Pinto, John A. *The Trevi Fountain.* New Haven and London: Yale University Press, 1986.

Pirenne, Henri. *Medieval Cities.* New York: Doubleday, 1956.

Plunz, Richard. "The Design Equation", in Plunz, Richard and Maria Paola Sutto, ed. *Urban Climate Change Crossroads*. New York: Urban Design Lab. 2008.

Ponting, Clive. *A Green History of the World*. New York: W.W. Norton. 2005.

Register, Richard. *EcoCities: Rebuilding Cities in Balance with Nature*. Gabriola Island, Canada: New Society Publishers; Revised edition 2006

Reichlin, Bruno. *Figures of Neorealism in Italian Architecture*. in Grey Room 06

Rifkin, Jeremy. *Entropy*. New York: Viking. 1980.

Rifkin, Jeremy. *The Hydrogen Economy*. Jeremy P Tarcher. 2004.

Robert Hughes. *Rome*. New York: Knopf. 2011.

Robert Maxwell. *The Two Way Stretch: Modernism, Tradition and Innovation*. London: Academy Editions. 1996

Robinson, O. F. *Ancient Rome: City Planning and Administration*. New York: Routledge. 1994.

Robinson, Sydney, ed. *The Continuous Present of Organic Architecture*. Cincinatti, OH: Contemporary Arts Center. 1991.

Rogers, Richard. *Cities for a Small Planet*. London: Faber and Faber, Ltd. 1997

Rosenzweig, Roy. "Wizards, Bureaucrats, Warriors, and Hackers: Writing the History of the Internet." in *American Historical Review 103* (1998).

Rossi Aldo, *A Scientific Autobiography*. Cambridge, MA: MIT Press, 1981.

Rossi Aldo, *Architecture of the City*. Cambridge, MA: MIT Press, 1982.

Rowe C., A. Koetter, *Collage City*, Cambridge, MA: MIT Press, 1978.

Rowe, Colin. "Transparency: Literal and Phenomenal." in *Perspecta*. 1963

Rowe, Colin. *The Mathematics of the Ideal Villa*. Cambridge, MA: MIT Press, 1982.

Rudofsky, Bernard. *Architecture without Architects: An Introduction to Non-Pedigreed Architecture*. New York: The Museum of Modern Art. 1964.

Rushkoff, Douglas. *Life, Inc*. NY: Random House, 2009.

Rykwert, Joseph. "Architecture is for Everyone". in Giulia Vola, ed. *Transmitting Architecture*. 2008.

Rykwert, Joseph. *The Idea of a Town: Anthropology of Urban Form in Rome, Italy and the Ancient World*. Cambridge, MA: MIT Press. 1988.

Safdie, Moshe, *The City After the Automobile*. New York: Harper Collins, 1997.

Sale, Kirkpatrick. *Christopher Columbus and the Conquest of Paradise*. London: Tauris Parke Paperbacks 2006.

Sant'Elia, Antonio and Filippo Tommaso Marinetti "Futurist Architecture" (1914) in Conrads, Ulrich, ed. *Programs and Manifestoes on 20th-Century Architecture*. Cambridge, MA: MIT Press. 1975

Sassen, Saskia. "Seeing Like a City" in Burdett, Ricky, ed. *The Endless City*. London: Phaidon. 2007.

Schezen, Roberto. *Roman Gardens: Villas of the City*. Milan: Monacelli Press. 2001.

Schumacher, E. F. *Small is Beautiful*. New York: Harper Colphon Books. 1973.

Scott, Felicity. "Bernard Rudofsky: Allegories of Nomadism and Dwelling." Goldhagen, Sarah Williams ed. *Anxious Modernisms: Experimentation in Postwar Architectural Culture*. Cambridge, MA: MIT Press. 2002.

Sear, F.. *Roman Architecture*. Ithaca: Cornell University Press. 1982

Sear, Frank. Roman Architecture. Ithaca: Cornell University Press. 1982.

Segarra Lagunes, Maria Margarita. *Il Tevere e Roma: Storia di una simbiosi*. Rome: Gangemi. 2004.

Sennet, Richard. "The Open City" in Burdett, Ricky, ed. *The Endless City*. London: Phaidon. 2007.

Sitte, Camillo. *City Planning According to Artistic Principles*. New York: Random House. 1901.

Soleri, Paolo. *Arcology: The City in the Image of Man*. Cambridge, MA: M.I.T. Press. 1969.

Speth, James. *Red Sky at Morning: America and the Crisis of the Global Environment*. New Haven: Yale University Press. 2005.

Spirn, Anne Whiston. *The Granite Garden: Urban Nature and Human Design*. New York: Basic Books. 1984.

Spirn, Anne Whiston. "The Legacy of Frederick Law Olmsted." in *Uncommon Ground*. 1995.

Stambaugh, J.E. *The Ancient Roman City*. Baltimore: Johns Hopkins University Press. 1988.

Stohr, Kate "100 Years of Humanitarian Design" in *Architects for Humanity*, ed. Design like you give a damn. New York: Metropolis Books. 2006.

Sullivan, George H. *Not Built in a Day: Exploring the Architecture of Rome*. New York: Caroll and Graff. 2006.

Taylor, Rabun. *Roman Builders: A Study in Architectural Process*. Cambridge, UK: Cambridge University Press. 2003.

Thompson, D'Arcy. *On Growth and Form*. Cambridge: Cambridge University Press. 1992 (first published 1917)

Tung, Anthony M. *Preserving the World's Great Cities. The Destruction and Renewal of the Historic Metropolis*. New York: Clarkson Potter. 2001. p. 29-50

Tzonis, Alexander and Liane Lefaivre. "Why critical regionalism today?" in *Theorizing a new agenda for architecture: an anthology of architectural theory 1965-1995*. Kate Nesbitt (ed.). New York: Princeton Architectural Press. 1990

Van Hinte, Ed, Marc Neelen, Jacques Vink, Piet Vollaard, ed. *Smart Architecture*. Rotterdam: 010 Publishers. 2003.

Venturi R., Scott Brown D., Izenour S., *Learning from Las Vegas*, Cambridge, MA: MIT Press, 1977.

Venturi Venturi Robert. *Complexity and Contradiction in Architecture*. New York: Museum of Modern Art. 1977.

Vidler, Anthony. "The Scenes of the Street" in Anderson, Stanford, ed. *On Streets*. Cambridge, MA: MIT Press, 1986.

Vidler, Anthony. *Histories of the Immediate Present: Inventing Architectural Modernism*. Cambridge, MA: MIT Press. 2008.

Viollet-le-Duc. *Discourses on Architecture*. Charleston, Nabu Press, 2011. First published 1875.

Vitruvius. *The Ten Books on Architecture*. translated by Morris Hicky Morgan. New York: Dover. 1960.

Vittorio Gregotti. *New Directions in Italian Architecture*. New York: George Braziller. 1968.

Wachsmann, Konrad. *The Turning Point of Building: Structure and Design*. New York: Reinhold. 1961.

Ward-Perkins, B. *Roman Imperial Architecture*. New Haven: The Yale University Press. 1981.

Weart, Spencer. *The Discovery of Global Warming*. Cambridge: Harvard University Press. 2008.

Weisman, Alan. *The World Without Us*. New York: Picador. 2007.

Welch, Evelyn. *Art in Renaissance Italy, 1350-1500*. Oxford: Oxford History of Art. 2001.

Wells, Malcolm. *Gentle Architecture*. New York: McGraw-Hill. 1982.

Welter, Volker. Biopolis: *Patrick Geddes and the City of Life*. Cambridge, MA: MIT Press. 2002.

Wheeler, Stephen M. and Timothy Beatley. *Planning for Sustainability in European Cities. The Sustainable Urban Development Reader*. London and New York: Routledge. 2004.

Whyte, William H. *The Social Life of Small Urban Spaces*. New York: Project for Public Spaces Inc. 1980.

Wiener, Norbert. *The Human Use of Human Beings: Cybernetics and Society*. Boston: Da Capo Press. 2008. (Originally published 1950)

Wigley, Mark. "Network Fever." in *Grey Room 4* (2001).

Wittkower, Rudolf. *Architectural Principles in the Age of Humanism*. John Wiley and Sons. 1998.

Wittkower, Rudolf. *Art and Architecture in Italy, 1600-1750*. New Haven: Yale University Press Pelican History of Art. 1999.

Wright, Frank Lloyd. *An Organic Architecture*. Cambridge: MIT Press. 1970. First published 1939.

Wurman, Richard Saul. *Information Anxiety 2*. Indianapolis: Que. 2001.

Yeang, Ken. *Bioclimatic Architecture*. London: Artemis. 1994.

ACKNOWLEDGEMENTS

For fueling my longstanding interest in sustainability and the city, my thanks go out to the late Paolo Soleri who stands with R. Buckminster Fuller at the head of a long list of 20th century urban thinkers who inspired this work. Early interest in Italy and its urban environments came from professors Steve Slaby, Tony Vidler, David Coffin and Robert Maxwell at Princeton, and Jorge Silvetti, Wilfried Wang, Marcel Meili, Joan Busquets, Rafael Moneo and many others at Harvard. My brilliant colleagues at Scala Reale and later Context Travel, especially Paul Bennett, provided feedback and fuel for thought throughout the project. In Rome, support and inspiration has come from a varied list of thinkers and architects, including Antonio Tamburrino, Carlo Gasparrini, Luca Zevi, Valeria Sassanelli, Livio de Santoli, Giovanni Caudo, Salvatore de Settis, Paolo Berdini, Carlo Cellamare, Lorenzo Romito, Giulia Fiocca, Mario Cucinella Massimiliano Fuksas, Stefano Boeri, Katherine Rinne, Pia Schneider, Cinzia Abbate, Carlo Vigevano, Alan Ceen, Scott Schlimgen, Dora Cirone and many, many others. For advice on the publishing world, I have been lucky to have words of encouragement from Rick Steves, Doug Rushkoff, Walter Kirn, Constance Hale, David Carr, Eric Tarloff and a long list of illustrious acquaintances. Thanks to my editor Rich Higgins for having been gentle and instructive in accompanying the manuscript into its final form. Thanks to interns, especially Emily Miller, who read my manuscript and gave valuable feedback.

And, of course, I thank my family, my wife Lucia, my sons John and Daniel who have grown up with this project, and my sisters Jenny and Elizabeth who provided valuable feedback and edits along the way.